CW01065245

JONATHAN BARDON was born in Dublin in
the High School Dublin, Trinity College D
Belfast and the University of Ulster, where he completed a Ph.D. in 1997.
His publications include *Belfast: An Illustrated History* (Blackstaff Press,
1982), *A History of Ulster* (Blackstaff Press, 1992), and *Belfast: A
Century* (Blackstaff Press, 1999).

Patent creating James Hamilton, Viscount Claneboye, and featuring
a coloured and gilded royal portrait of James I, 4 May [1622]

A Guide to

LOCAL HISTORY
SOURCES

in the

PUBLIC RECORD OFFICE
OF NORTHERN IRELAND

JONATHAN BARDON

Public Record Office
of Northern Ireland

THE
BLACKSTAFF
PRESS

BELFAST

The cover is made up from documents, photographs and maps held
in the Public Record Office of Northern Ireland

First published in 2000 by
The Blackstaff Press Limited
Blackstaff House, Wildflower Way, Apollo Road
Belfast BT12 6TA, Northern Ireland
for the Public Record Office of Northern Ireland

Printed in Ireland by Betaprint

A CIP catalogue record for this book
is available from the British Library

ISBN 0-85640-671-6

CONTENTS

PREFACE

I am delighted to introduce you to this book, which is a working companion volume to *Tracing Your Ancestors in Northern Ireland* (The Stationery Office, 1997) written by Ian Maxwell and edited by Grace McGrath. That well-received publication has established itself as a practical guide for those undertaking family history research in the Public Record Office of Northern Ireland (PRONI).

The author of this volume, Jonathan Bardon, is a writer of note. In recent years he has both informed and entertained his many readers with titles including *A History of Ulster* (Blackstaff Press, 1992) and *Belfast: An Illustrated History* (Blackstaff Press, 1982). He now brings his fluent style of writing to a guide to investigating and researching local history in Ulster, using sources available in PRONI. Recognising the need for a professional-looking and well-illustrated book, the author and PRONI attracted the publishing services of the Blackstaff Press, which, among many other accolades, won the *Sunday Times* Small Publisher of the Year award in 1992. The result is a publication that will be an essential tool for anyone seeking to re-create an accurate picture of how our ancestors lived, worshipped and worked. It is essentially a key to unlock some of the mass of manuscript treasures housed in PRONI and it brings with it a promise of interesting, enjoyable and rewarding research.

As the Permanent Secretary of the Department of Culture, Arts and Leisure, I head up a department with a remit that includes archives, libraries and museums. I am therefore particularly pleased that this publication contains extensive references to the complementary local history sources in Northern Ireland's libraries and museums. Co-operation across the three disciplines promises to make invaluable heritage assets more readily accessible to a wider public, and I welcome this publication as a major contribution to that strategy of co-operation and collaboration.

Aideen McGinley
PERMANENT SECRETARY
DEPARTMENT OF CULTURE, ARTS AND LEISURE

PRONI'S PUBLIC SERVICES

POSTAL ENQUIRIES

Although PRONI staff are able to provide advice and will answer limited and specific enquiries, they cannot carry out research on behalf of enquirers. It is not their responsibility.

All correspondence should be addressed to:

THE PUBLIC RECORD OFFICE OF NORTHERN IRELAND
66 Balmoral Avenue
BELFAST BT9 6NY

TELEPHONE ENQUIRIES

If you wish to consult the records, especially if you have some distance to travel, it is advisable to write to the office in advance to ascertain whether relevant records are available for consultation:

TEL: 028 9025 5905
FAX: 028 9025 5999
e-mail: proni@nics.gov.uk

PRONI ON THE INTERNET

PRONI has had a presence on the World Wide Web since 1995 and the site has grown and developed since then. There are now some 35 million bytes of information, the equivalent of approximately eight thousand A4 pages, available for downloading. This information is available twenty-four hours a day to anyone around the world who has access to a computer which is linked to the internet.

Website address: http://proni.nics.gov.uk/index.htm

PRONI OUTREACH CENTRES

If you are planning a visit to PRONI and you live some distance away from Belfast, then you should make use of a number of our outreach centres, which are situated throughout Northern Ireland. The following organisations host these centres:

Harbour Museum
Derry City Council
Harbour Square
LONDONDERRY BT48 6AF
TEL: 028 7137 7331
FAX: 028 7137 7633
e-mail: tower.museum@derrycity.gov.uk

Armagh Ancestry
Armagh District Council
St Patrick's Trian
38a English Street
ARMAGH BT61 7BA
TEL: 028 3752 1802
FAX: 028 3751 0033
e-mail: ancestry@acdc.btinternet
WEBSITE:http://www.armagh.gov.uk

Border Counties History Collective
Main Street
Blacklion
County Cavan
TEL: 00 353 72 53440
FAX: 00 353 72 53409
e-mail: bchc@eircom.net
WEBSITE:http://homepage.eircom.net/~historycollective/

Morrow's Shop Museum
Ballymena Borough Council
13–15 Bridge Street
BALLYMENA BT43 5EJ
TEL: 028 2565 3663

These outreach facilities contain a range of PRONI searching aids (for example, computerised subject and geographical indexes), an interactive touchscreen video, and locally relevant catalogue lists.

VISITING PRONI

On your arrival at PRONI's reception area, your name and address and the purpose of your visit (for example, local history research) will be recorded on the computerised registration system, and you will be given a Reader's Ticket. No bags, overcoats, briefcases, et cetera, are allowed into the Public Search Room, and these must be left in the locker provided. Admission is free.

Immediately after registration, first-time visitors will be greeted in the waiting area by a member of staff from the Public Search Room, who will take details of their topic of research and help them to get started. An interactive video located in the waiting area introduces visitors to the wide range of records deposited at PRONI, while at the same time demonstrating some of the work that goes on behind the scenes to preserve the records and make them available to the public.

ACCESS TO THE RECORDS

The 'thirty-year-rule' governs access to official records in Northern Ireland as elsewhere in the United Kingdom. In essence this means that a record – file, minute book, et cetera – is *elegible* for release thirty years from the date of its last paper. Following a 'sensitivity review', most official material is made available to the public for consultation.

Private depositors are not bound by the 'thirty-year-rule', and have tended to apply different restrictions on access to their records. However, private depositors are now being encouraged to rationalise and/or establish terms of access to Northern Ireland's archival heritage so as to '. . . ensure public access to that heritage which fully meets Open Government standards'.

ANNUAL CLOSURE

The Public Search Room and Reading Rooms are open to the public from 9.15am to 4.45pm, Monday to Friday (late-night opening on Thursdays until 8.45pm), except on public holidays and for two weeks' stocktaking, which usually takes place during the last week in November and the first week in December.

GROUP VISITS

Group visits are welcome, but **must** be arranged in advance – contact the Reader Services Section at the above address. In order to get the maximum benefit from a visit, it is worth taking the trouble to consider exactly what you want your group to gain from visiting PRONI. Then put your ideas to one of our Reader Services staff who can help and advise you.

PHOTOCOPIES

PRONI provides a photocopying service as far as is practical – ask our Reader Services staff for details of reprographic fees and charges.

There are some documents, however, that will **not** be photocopied. These include: documents in guard books, as there is a risk of damage to the volume when it is upended; outsize documents or the contents of outsize volumes (that is, larger than A3); parchments, parts of maps, and photographic prints; fragile volumes (that is, where there is a risk of the spine breaking); and press cuttings in scrapbooks if these are folded and difficult to handle without damage.

Copies of Ordnance Survey maps can be ordered. These may take up to ten working days to process.

Where original archives have been microfilmed, the microfilm copy rather than the original documents will be made available; only microfilm print-outs (rather than photocopies) will be supplied in order to save wear and tear on the original records.

RESTAURANT

Situated at the side of the building, the restaurant offers a choice of hot and cold meals, sandwiches, and a range of beverages.

VISITORS WHO ARE DISABLED

Wheelchair access is available at the main entrance and at the restaurant. A toilet, specially adapted to accommodate wheelchairs, is located in the reception area.

HOW TO FIND US

By train: the nearest station is Balmoral
By bus from the city centre: the number 59, Lisburn Road, and the number 71, Malone Road
By car: from the M1 use the Balmoral exit

1
BEGINNING YOUR RESEARCH

Embarking on historical research for the first time can be exciting and absorbing, but at the same time it can lead to frustration in the search for direction and meaningful clues. Evidence is the raw material for every historian, but it is generally best to begin by finding out what evidence has been turned up by others and how it has been interpreted. This means consulting books, pamphlets and articles in journals which seem relevant to the topic under investigation.

It could be that the nearest public library to the locality to be researched has the volumes you need; local librarians, delighted to encounter someone not enquiring after a much-sought-after thriller, can often provide useful guidance and arrange inter-library loans. All the education and library boards hold specialist Irish and local studies collections at their headquarters. For example, Belfast Central Library has the impressive Bigger Collection on the second floor which includes some very rare volumes (these are for consultation only). Omagh Branch Library, to give another example, has an Irish and local studies collection housing some five thousand volumes as well as considerable holdings of maps, microfilms, journals and newspapers relating particularly to County Tyrone. The Linen Hall Library, in Donegall Square North, Belfast, is justifiably renowned for its collection of local studies books, pamphlets, old newspapers and manuscripts – not to speak of its unique Political Collection on material relating to events in Northern Ireland since 1968, including much ephemera. Those with access to the Queen's University Library can consult the renowned Henry Collection of books on Irish history. No serious researcher should be without the pocket-sized but

PLAN OF THE PUBLIC SEARCH ROOM

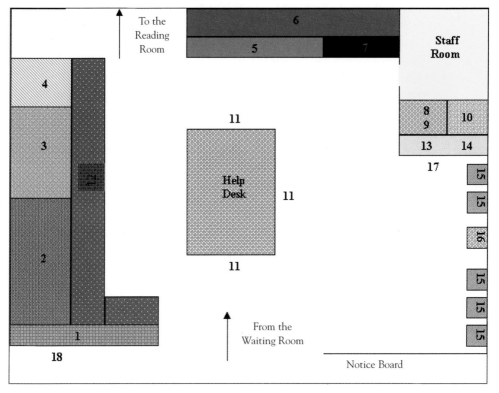

1   BLUE CALENDARS – privately deposited original records (REF D/ . . .)
2   BROWN CALENDARS – departmental records (that is, records of central government departments)
3   GREY CALENDARS – non-departmental records, including schools, local authorities, public bodies and courts
4   PRONI guides to records (for example, annual deposits and releases, guide to church records, et cetera)
5   GREEN CALENDARS – microfilm copies (including 1901 census, church records, films and tapes) (REF MIC/ . . .)
6   RED CALENDARS – photocopies of transcripts of privately deposited papers (REF T/ . . .)
7   BLACK CALENDARS – church records, including diocesan records
8   HOUSEHOLDERS' INDEX
9   GRIFFITH'S VALUATION
10 REFERENCE BOOKS – for example, Deputy Keeper's Reports
11 STREET DIRECTORIES, and various reference books
12 PERSONAL NAME INDEX
13 PLACE NAMES INDEX
14 PRE-1900 WILLS
15 COMPUTER TERMINALS (document ordering)
16 PUBLICATIONS STAND
17 LEAFLET STAND
18 MANUAL SUBJECT AND GEOGRAPHICAL INDEXES

information-packed volume, *Ulster Libraries: Archives, Museums and Ancestral Heritage Centres* by Robert K. O'Neill (Ulster Historical Foundation, 1997).

There are more than ninety local history societies affiliated to the Federation for Ulster Local Studies (FULS). Their lecture and field trip programmes may be relevant to your interests and, in addition to local histories written by members, many of them publish journals, including: *The Glynns*, journal of the Glens of Antrim Historical Society; *Concordia*, journal of the Strabane History Society; and the *Clogher Record*, journal of the cross-border Clogher Historical Society. *Local History Link*, a newsletter issued by FULS, provides up-to-date information on journals, local history publications and associated events. Academic journals may seem dauntingly specialist but they often include invaluable articles on local topics. The best-known include: *Irish Historical Studies, Irish Economic and Social History, Proceedings of the Royal Irish Academy, Ulster Folklife,* and *Journal of the Royal Society of Antiquaries of Ireland.* A particularly useful reference book is *The Oxford Companion to Irish History,* edited by S.J. Connolly (Oxford, 1998). Geography Publications has embarked on an ambitious project to publish a volume for each county in Ireland on its history, society and literature; the first volumes published for Ulster were Down, Donegal and Londonderry.

Lists of local histories on places in Ulster are too numerous to be listed here as they would fill a large volume; if you do not have a title or an author, consult placenames in library catalogues. Useful Guides include: *Pathways to Ulster's Past: Sources and Resources for Local Studies* by Peter Collins (Institute of Irish Studies, 1998); *Doing Irish Local History: Pursuit and Practice,* edited by Raymond Gillespie and Myrtle Hill (Institute of Irish Studies, 1998); *Tracing the Past* by William Nolan (Blackrock, 1982); and *Townlands in Ulster: Local History Studies,* edited by W.H. Crawford and R.H. Foy (Ulster Historical Foundation and Federation for Ulster Local Studies, 1998). A *Dictionary of Ulster Place-Names* by Patrick McKay (Institute of Irish Studies, 1999) explains around 1,300 names in the nine counties of Ulster and is replete with lucid explanation. Other publications relevant to particular aspects of local history will be referred to in subsequent chapters of this guide.

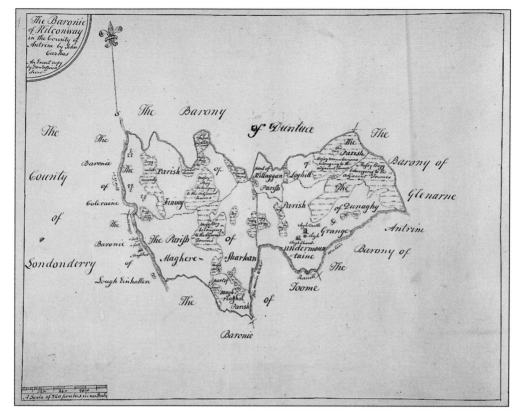

Petty's map of the barony of Glenarm, County Antrim, c. 1655

D/597/2/64

2
ADMINISTRATIVE DIVISIONS

KINGDOMS AND LORDSHIPS

Until the close of Elizabeth I's reign in 1603 it could not be said that all of Ireland was contained in one kingdom. Chroniclers listed high kings of Ireland going back to very early times but it is likely that these rulers in pre-Christian and early Christian centuries held positions which were largely honorific. It was only after the Viking raids at the end of the eighth century that certain powerful provincial kings made serious attempts to assert mastery over the whole island. The first to come close to success was Brian Boru, slain at the moment of victory at Clontarf in 1014. Several of his successors, the O'Briens, and later the O'Connors of Connacht, won wide acknowledgement of their claim to high kingship but all ruled, in the words of the annalists, *co fresabra*, that is 'with opposition'. It was the opposition of Dermot MacMurrough, king of Leinster, to high king Rory O'Connor which led on directly to the Norman invasion of 1169.

Both before and after the coming of the Normans there were dozens of kingdoms in Ireland. A typical kingdom was the size of a barony (see below) and indeed several baronies, such as Iveagh in County Down (from Uí Eachach Cobha), were named from them. The smallest type of kingdom was the *tuath* (cognate with the words 'teutonic' and 'Deutsch') and by the time Christianity was being brought to Ireland these small kingdoms were loosely ruled by over-kings. For example, the kingdom of Uladh from which Ulster is named (*Uladh tír*, the land of the Ulaidh), comprising the present counties of Antrim and Down, was the over-kingdom of the following kingdoms in the ninth century: Dál Riata, Dál nAraide, Latharna, Uí Eachach Cobha, Dál Fiatach, Uí Eachach Arda and Leth Cathail – the localities of Dalriada, Larne, the Ards peninsula and Lecale are named from four of these. The Uí Néill supremacy of Tír Eóghain in mid-Ulster gave its name to County Tyrone. Unlike the province of Connacht, Ulster was never welded together to form a provincial kingdom.

As the Normans spread over parts of the island, Gaelic kings and kingdoms gradually disappeared to be replaced by lords and lordships. The shapes and fortunes of lordships changed constantly; some disappeared and others were newly created. For example, most of the modern counties of Antrim and Down were conquered by the Norman freebooters John de Courcy and Hugh de Lacy, and were then taken over by the English Crown in the thirteenth century to become the earldom of Ulster. In the fourteenth and fifteenth centuries the earldom was over-run in stages by a branch of Tyrone O'Neills, Clann Aodha Buidhe (the family of yellow-haired Hugh), to create the Gaelic lordship of Clandeboye, as the English called it.

Henry II came to Ireland in 1171 and annexed the island for his Angevin dominions. In practice this 'lordship of Ireland' included only the territory conquered by the Normans and the English. Some barons named their conquests 'lordships' and anglicised the Gaelic territorial names to become, for example, Meath, Desmond, Thomond, and Ulster. After a peak at the end of the thirteenth century, the authority of the English crown contracted to coastal towns and an area around Dublin known as the Pale. By the mid-fifteenth century, for example, the Crown was left only with Carrickfergus and portions of Lecale in the province of Ulster.

The Battle of Bosworth in 1485 marked the beginning of the Tudor recovery in Ireland but it was not until the end of the Nine Years War (1594–1603) – when a coalition of Gaelic lords in Ulster fought the Crown – that the island was conquered from end to end. James I was the first ruler of England, Scotland, Wales and Ireland, though it was Henry VIII in 1541 who changed the title 'lordship of Ireland' to the 'kingdom of Ireland'.

COUNTIES

King John, created Lord of Ireland by his father Henry II, began the process of shiring conquered lands in Ireland to assert the authority of the Crown and of common law by appointing sheriffs. By the end of the fifteenth century most progress had been made in the province of Leinster and all attempts so far to shire parts of Ulster had failed completely.

By 1579 all of the provinces of Leinster, Munster and Connacht had been shired, and in Ulster the lands east of the River Bann had been made into the counties of Antrim and Down. In 1585 Sir John Perrott created the counties of Donegal, Fermanagh, Armagh, Cavan, Tyrone, Monaghan and Coleraine, and he fixed a new frontier for Ulster by detaching Louth and adding Cavan. During the launch of the Ulster Plantation in 1610, James I created the new county of Londonderry from Perrott's county of Coleraine with the addition of the barony of Loughinsholin (taken from Tyrone), Derry (soon to become the walled city of Londonderry), land on the west bank of the Foyle (taken from Donegal), and land on the east bank of the Lower Bann river sur-rounding Coleraine (taken from Antrim) – this was to make the area more attractive to the rather unenthusiastic London Companies who had agreed to plant what was then generally referred to by the English as 'O'Cahan's Country'.

Counties were judicial areas presided over by grand juries. These juries, made up of men of property, increased their local government functions in the eighteenth and nineteenth centuries until the Local Government Act of 1898, which replaced them with county councils. Counties remain important administrative units in the Republic of Ireland, but in Northern Ireland since 1972 their administrative func-tions have been taken over by education and library boards, health boards, district councils and centralised bodies such as the Northern Ireland Housing Executive.

BARONIES

The barony, a unit of landownership introduced by the Normans, is best considered to be a subdivision of a county, though some baronies overlapped more than one county. In the twentieth century baronies no longer have any functions left to them but they can be important to the local historian as they often mark the frontiers of Gaelic kingdoms at the time of the conquest and because thereafter they served a significant role; in the seventeenth century, the Civil Survey and the Down Survey used the barony as the main unit for describing and mapping estates, confiscated or otherwise; the role of the barony was enhanced in the eighteenth century by the authority to levy cess to pay for road building approved by the grand jury; the barony was a legal division where quarter sessions were held; and the barony was a significant valuation and census subdivision in the nineteenth century.

PARISHES

Dioceses (areas over which bishops had authority) did not have administrative functions either in Gaelic or in English-ruled Ireland. It was not until 1320 that the boundaries were recorded (for the purpose of an ecclesiastical taxation) and thereafter alterations were made from time to time. Dioceses in Ulster in 1320 were: Raphoe; Derry; Connor; Down; Dromore; Armagh; Clogher; and Kilmore.

Parishes did have an administrative role: the smallest religious divisions of the Church, they were taken over by the Established Church – that is, the reformed Anglican Church – in the sixteenth century and given functions in the government of the country by Dublin Castle. Most parishes were created in early Christian times though they fitted very uncomfortably into Gaelic Ireland, since there were no proper towns on the island at all until the Vikings made permanent settlements, and the parish was supposed to be centred on a town. For the local historian, it is important to realise that: in the seventeenth century the parish was a pivotal unit in both the Civil Survey and the Down Survey; the civil parish was the unit used for the levying of tithe (the Tithe Composition books which survive from the early nineteenth century are of great value); the parish was the territory chosen for the detailed descriptions given in the Ordnance Survey Memoirs; and the parish was used as a census and a valuation unit.

Catholic parishes after the Reformation were large for the populations they served but as penal restrictions were lifted more parishes were created but they were never given civil administrative functions except in education.

TOWNLANDS

The importance of the townland to the local historian in Ireland is difficult to exaggerate, particularly in Ulster, because it was used for the allocation of estates in the Plantation. 'Townland' is a rough translation of *baile* (usually anglicised as 'bally') which, though it means 'town' today, meant 'settlement' in the past. The Irish tended to measure their land at a local level not by area but by value. High-quality farmland was divided into many small townlands while rough grazing and poor bogland formed large townlands by comparison.

When territory was confiscated in the seventeenth century it made good sense for the London government to specify townlands in grants since these were immediately understood by the native population at a time when surveys by Thomas Raven and others were not accompanied by accurate mapping. From this time onwards, landlords almost always let their estates by townland and townlands feature prominently on estate maps and in rentals. The townland was used in the nineteenth century as a valuation area in the Tithe Composition Books and as an enumeration unit in the census and in Griffith's Valuation.

The very names of townlands are valuable to the local historian as they indicate physical features, land use and previous ownership. For example, Ballymoney is a townland name appearing in many counties: it means the 'townland of the bog', and the very widely distributed name Leitrim means 'grey slope'. In the counties of Antrim and Down townland names can indicate Norman manors such as Ballyrobert (formerly 'Robertiston' or Robert's town) and Ballywalter ('Waltirton' or Walter's town) in the Six Mile Water valley, and Ballywalter ('Talbotiston' or Talbot's town) on the Ards peninsula.

The number of townlands was never static: as the population rose in the eighteenth and early nineteenth centuries new ones were created by landowners, such as the Earl of Antrim, and by the Ordnance Survey. At present there are about 62,000 townlands in Ireland, and about 9,700 in Ulster. In Northern Ireland townland names are recognised as postal addresses by the Post Office only in County Fermanagh. Useful reference works include: *Townlands in Ulster*, edited by W.H. Crawford (1998), the series *Place-Names of Northern Ireland*, edited by Gerard Stockman (volume I is *County Down I: Newry and South-West*

Down by Gregory Toner and Micheál B. Ó Mainnín, 1992) and 'The study of townlands in Ulster' by W.H. Crawford in *Doing Irish History*, edited by Raymond Gillespie and Myrtle Hill. The PRONI guide leaflet, *Local History 1: The Townland*, can be obtained in the Public Search Room.

POOR LAW UNIONS

The introduction, with some minor alterations, of the new Poor Law into Ireland in 1838 created Poor Law Unions. Townlands (not parishes as in England) were grouped together to form an administrative unit to provide relief to the destitute centred on a workhouse built in the largest market town. At the outset there were 130 unions in Ireland. This was the first step towards representative local government in the countryside as the Boards of Guardians, with the authority given to them to strike a rate and to administer relief, was – unlike grand juries – elected by ratepayers. Minutes of the Boards of Guardians provide graphic evidence on the impact of the Great Famine in different areas and Poor Law valuations yield detailed information on the economy of localities in the nineteenth century. In Northern Ireland the unions retained a significant role in the twentieth century, providing an insight, for example, on the impact of the 1930s depression in Belfast and Newry.

RECENT ADMINISTRATIVE DIVISIONS

Members of the Irish parliament (dissolved by the Act of Union in 1801) were elected from counties, incorporated boroughs and Trinity College Dublin. The Union created new electoral divisions which were periodically revised. The 1920 Government of Ireland Act set up multi-member constituencies, accepted in the Irish Free State in 1922 but replaced by single-member constituencies in 1929 in Northern Ireland. Up to 1972 Northern Ireland had parliamentary constituencies for its devolved parliament in Belfast in addition to ones which returned members to Westminster. After 1972 multi-member electoral areas were created to return representatives to a variety of assemblies. Boundaries of constituencies are revised periodically to take account of changes in the distribution of the region's population.

After the suspension of devolved government in Northern Ireland in

1972, city corporations, county councils, town councils and rural district councils were replaced by Belfast City Council, Derry City Council and twenty-six district councils, all of which exercised less authority than the bodies they replaced. Education was administered by education and library boards; health by health boards; public housing by the Northern Ireland Housing Executive; and other functions by departments of government, such as the Department of the Environment, and by government agencies such as the Rate Collection Agency. In all of these bodies elected representatives are outnumbered by appointed and co-opted members. The Northern Ireland Assembly, elected in 1998 from multi-member electoral areas, is expected to bring changes to these boards and agencies.

Portion of Rocque's map of Ireland, showing St Patrick's Purgatory and its immediate hinterland, 1794   D/754/6/1

3
MAPS

Almost every local history study begins with maps. You could start by getting the latest edition of the Ordnance Survey map of your area and make photocopies of it on which you could mark in additional information thrown up by your research. For example, by looking at successive editions of the six-inch-to-the-mile OS maps you can record changes which have taken place since the years just before the Famine when the first editions were published. To go back further in time you could look at estate maps commissioned by landowners in the eighteenth and nineteenth centuries, and finally at seventeenth-century survey maps and at maps produced during the Plantation and the Elizabethan conquest which preceded it.

SIXTEENTH-CENTURY MAPS

Until the sixteenth century few maps of any value were made in Ireland. One fifteenth-century map of the island, for example, shows Lough Derg, a small lake in south-east County Donegal then known throughout Europe as a place of pilgrimage, as by far the largest sheet of freshwater in Ireland. The recovery and extension of the English Crown's authority in Ireland under the Tudors, the emergence of the threat from Spain, and the protracted military campaigns needed to crush the resistance of the Gaelic lords, created an urgent requirement for accurate maps at a time when the craft of cartography was making great strides forward. Sixteenth-century maps of Ulster in particular reveal how little Tudor governments knew of the province west of the River Bann.

   Most sixteenth-century maps are held in the British Library, London, the Public Record Office at Kew, the National Library in Dublin, Trinity College Dublin, and in other repositories in Oxford, London and Dublin, but PRONI has copies of nearly all of these.

EXAMPLES INCLUDE

1580	Baptista Boazio's map of Ulster	T/2528/5
c. 1580	map of mid-Ulster	T/1493/50
1587	map of mid-Ulster, showing lands divided between Turlough Luineach O'Neill and Hugh, Earl of Tyrone	T/1493/51
1599	map of the north of Ireland by Baptista Boazio	T/1518/6
1599–1600	map with description of the Earl of Essex's encampment during his campaign to the frontier of Ulster	T/1518/7/8
c. 1600	map of Ulster by Francis Jobson	T/1669/4

SEVENTEENTH-CENTURY MAPS

The closing phases of the Nine Years War, which resulted in the conquest of the entire province of Ulster by the Crown for the first time, led to the drawing of attractive and increasingly accurate maps. The finest of these were by Richard Barthelet, eventually killed on campaign in County Donegal, who included coloured sketches of encampments, engagements and castles inset in his maps.

EXAMPLES

> *c.* 1602   map of southern and mid-Ulster by Barthelet, including illustrations of an attack on a crannog, the coronation chair of the O'Neills at Tullahogue and Dungannon Castle (T/1244/11)
>
> *c.* 1602   map of River Blackwater valley with fortified positions by Barthelet (T/1244/13)
>
> *c.* 1602   map of the north-west of Ireland, collected and observed by Captain John Baxter and finished by Boazio (T/1518/3/A–B)

THE PLANTATION OF ULSTER

The confiscations which followed the Treaty of Mellifont in 1603, the Flight of the Earls in 1607 and Sir Cahir O'Doherty's rebellion in 1608 greatly increased the demand for maps. The government needed to know the location and extent of the lands they had escheated to allocate grants to undertakers, servitors, 'deserving' Irish, the Established Church and Trinity College Dublin. Very attractive though these maps are, they are not based on measured surveys but on inquisitions and other investigations. Irish land divisions feature prominently since grants specified these – anglicised as 'townlands', 'tates' and 'ballyboes' – and vagueness about acreage made it difficult to implement the terms of colonisation in many instances. However, the Plantation maps produced (for the most part by Thomas Raven and Sir Josias Bodley) contain vital information for the local historian and, meanwhile, other cartographers such as John Speede published maps raised to new standards of accuracy.

These maps are widely dispersed in British and Irish repositories but copies are available in PRONI.

EXAMPLES

> *c.* 1609   plantation maps for baronies in the escheated counties of Armagh, Cavan, Donegal, Fermanagh and south Londonderry by Sir Josias Bodley (T/2543/24)
>
> 1610   Speede's printed map of the province of Ulster with Enniskillen fort inset (T/1388)

1615   Maps and plans of the Drapers' Company proportion in County Londonderry – this collection includes maps of the estates up to the twentieth century (D/3632P/1–33)

THE CROMWELLIAN CONFISCATIONS

Following the rebellion of 1641 and the Confederacy Wars, Cromwell's government made sweeping land confiscations, mostly granted to soldiers and 'adventurers' from the City of London who had funded the parliamentarian campaign in Ireland. A 'civil survey' was commissioned by the government to describe each parish with named owners of land, details of land quality, acreage and boundaries. This great undertaking was completed for the province of Ulster, with the exception of the barony of Farney in County Monaghan. The survey was by inquisition only, information being collected from baronial juries. A fire in 1711 and then the destruction of the Public Record Office in Dublin in 1922 led to the loss of this survey but copies survive for the counties of Donegal, Londonderry and Tyrone.

Associated with the civil survey was the 'Downe' survey (so called because the information was laid *down* in maps) of Church, Crown and forfeited lands carried out by Sir William Petty. By now standards of accuracy were rising but for such a vast undertaking detailed measurement was not possible.

c. 1654   Petty's Downe Survey (copy)   T/2313/1/20–22

ESTATE MAPS

After the Restoration in 1660 more surveys were carried out to detail land ownership, quality of the soil, physical features, et cetera. The Books of Survey and Distribution were compiled around 1680 to calculate quit rent to be paid each year to the Crown under the terms of the Act of Settlement and Explanation. They give information on who had estates confiscated, who obtained land grants, and who were the principal landowners between 1641 and 1680. A version of the Books survive for all nine counties of Ulster in the Annesley papers(D/1854/1/23).

By this stage land owners were beginning to commission the making of maps of their estates. During the long period of peace which followed the close of the Williamite Wars the population rose, lands previously described as 'waste' were brought into cultivation and the domestic linen industry flourished, particularly in mid-Ulster. Landlords developed towns and markets and, through the grand juries, promoted road and bridge building. Such progress stimulated the demand for maps. PRONI has a very impressive collection of manuscript maps, to be found in estate papers, which are a vital resource for local historians researching the late seventeenth century and the eighteenth and nineteenth centuries. Earlier vague estimates, such as 'about a Muskett Shott', gave way to more accurate measuring by a more general use of the theodolite and of chaining. For example, William Starrat's maps of the Abercorn estate distinguished types of land, turf bogs, farm patterns, common land, field names, loughs, roads, woods, bridges, canals, dams, windmills and building details including the number of chimneys and whether or not roofs were thatched or slated. Owners sometimes mapped towns, including Downpatrick in 1729 and Armagh in 1767.

EXAMPLES

c. 1750   map of Hamiltonsbawn demesne, the estate of Sir Hans Hamilton, surveyed by Matthew Black (D/1606/6B/3)

1718–*c.* 1740   maps of the property of the Corry family, later Earls of Belmore, in and near the demesne at Castle Coole, surveyed by James Mortimer and James Thompson (T/3027)

1769–74   about sixty maps of the Earl of Ely's estate in the manors of Drumrose, Ardgart, Tully and Moyglass by Richard Frizell (D/580/121–181, 319 and 327)

1745   map of Ballymore Manor, County Armagh, part of the Duke of Manchester's estate, by Patrick Dougan (D/720/1)

1767   map of the City of Armagh surveyed for the primate by Robert Livingstone (T/2521/5)

1751–1841   maps of the Brownlow estates in County Armagh (D/1928/P/1–7)

The commissioning of maps often coincided with the expiration of leases, the arrival of a new agent or the coming of age of an heir (in 1734, for example, when the Earl of Antrim inherited his title).

Meanwhile maps on a larger scale were being made and printed for sale, one of the finest examples being a map of County Armagh by John Rocque in 1760 (T/1513/1). Major projects, such as the construction of canals, were often preceded by the commissioning of special-purpose maps, such as a 1703 map of the route of a proposed canal between Newry and Portadown (D/695/M/1).

The free PRONI guide leaflet, *Local History 4: The Books of Survey and Distribution*, can be obtained in the Public Search Room.

ORDNANCE SURVEY MAPS

The Ordnance Survey was set up in 1791 with headquarters first in the Tower of London and later in Southampton. In 1801 Kent was the first county to be surveyed but between 1824 and 1841 the survey concentrated on Ireland, partly because of anxiety about unrest on the island (as the name implies, the original purpose of the Ordnance Survey was military). The main stated purpose, however, was that Ireland's local taxation system – based on property values – was in need of reform. A precise measurement of townlands and a detailed valuation of lands and buildings were required because of previous inaccuracies, inconsistencies and omissions.

In 1824 a committee chaired by Thomas Spring Rice MP recommended a survey of the whole island at a scale of six inches to one mile. Richard Griffith, an eminent geologist, was put in charge of a new boundary department and the measuring was to be done by the Ordnance Survey, directed by Lieutenant-Colonel Thomas Colby. Colby, based in Mountjoy House in the Phoenix Park in Dublin, found himself in charge of the most advanced mapping operation undertaken up to that time anywhere in the world. At one stage over two thousand army officers and men, and civil assistants were involved. The Lough Foyle baseline was completed in 1828: it took sixty days and seventy men under the direction of Captain Thomas Drummond to carry out the operation – in 1960 it was discovered that the calculation was only one inch out.

The finished manuscript map (known as the 'fair plan') was compiled on a parish basis. Starting with Ulster, the whole of Ireland was mapped between 1825 and 1842. Engraving began in 1827 but it was only from 1835 that field boundaries were included, thus excluding most Ulster parishes. The boundary department supplied townland names and Colby also used government and estate records, and word-of-mouth evidence from clergy and land agents. Linguistic research was carried out by the great Gaelic scholar, John O'Donovan.

The first maps were printed in 1833 and by 1846 the publication of the first edition of six-inch maps for the whole country was completed: Ireland had been surveyed and mapped with a degree of thoroughness and accuracy unique for its time in the world. Revision of the early six-inch maps began before the first edition was finished. In this revised edition the boundaries of all townlands, civil parishes, baronies and counties were delineated for the first time. Antiquities and man-made items such as field outlines, roads and settlement features are shown. Maps were revised at first by cancelling obsolete information and by penning in fresh detail. For the second edition a complete resurvey was ordered: six-inch revisions for Ulster counties were published between 1853 and 1861, again between 1903 and 1906, and finally between 1921 and 1939. In 1898 copper plates were replaced by zinc, which resulted in thicker lines, larger lettering and symbols placed further apart. From the 1950s a new series, known as the Irish Grid, superseded the six-inch county maps.

When the Ordnance Survey began its work, it was appreciated that the valuation of towns and cities would require larger scale maps. At first there was no policy as to what scale should be adopted or what towns should be mapped. Some plans were prepared at twelve inches to the mile, some at twenty-four, and Belfast was surveyed at three chains to the inch (1:2376), and some important towns were not mapped at all. In 1832 the Valuation Office asked the Ordnance Survey to supply plans, at four feet to the mile (soon after changed to five inches), and around a hundred towns were mapped by 1842. Of these, only the map for Dublin was published, but copies of those relevant to Northern Ireland have been deposited in PRONI. The twenty-four-inch plan of Londonderry was revised in 1847 and Belfast was resurveyed in 1854. Plans of Belfast, Lurgan and Portadown were engraved and put on sale.

In 1857 it was decided to bring Ireland into line with Britain by surveying all Irish towns at ten inches to the mile, though this scheme was modified for some towns following complaints from the Valuation Office that the scale was too large. These maps are extraordinarily detailed showing, for example, flower beds, garden paths, isolated trees and interior walls – details which were omitted from the late 1870s. In 1893 the largest scale for all future OS maps was fixed at 1:2500, twenty-five inches to the mile. Some larger maps were produced for the Valuation Office but these were merely photographic enlargements.

In 1887 the decision was made to resurvey the whole island at twenty-five inches to the mile. Each block of sixteen 1:2500 sheets fitted four-by-four into one old six-inch sheet. This survey did not reach Ulster until the early 1900s and revisions continued up to the 1960s when these maps were gradually replaced by the Irish Grid series which in 1968 transferred to the to the 1:10,000 scale. The demand for small-scale came first from the railway commissioners. The first quarter-inch maps appeared in 1839; one-inch maps became available from 1855, most of them with hill shading most attractively engraved in hachures; and half-inch maps were published from 1911 onwards. Digital mapping was introduced in 1981–3 which, with the use of aerial photography, space technology and electronic distance measuring instruments, has made possible continuous revision and the production of a very wide range of special purpose maps.

The Ordnance Survey classification scheme in PRONI is as follows:

OS/1   first edition OS maps, 1830–4:

OS/1/1   maps for County Antrim
OS/1/2   maps for County Armagh
OS/1/3   maps for County Down
OS/1/4   maps for County Fermanagh
OS/1/5   maps for County Londonderry
OS/1/6   maps for County Tyrone

These maps are arranged by sheet number. For example, OS/1/2/1 is sheet 1 for County Armagh. To locate the relevant map for a townland you should look up the name of the townland in the Topographical Dictionary which will give you the appropriate six-inch sheet and the county. For example, the townland of Dunrevan is in County Tyrone and is to be found on sheet 16, so the PRONI reference will be OS/1/6/16 using the above formula. To locate the relevant map or maps for a larger area you will need to know the county. Consult the appropriate county index sheet in the Public Search Room or order out the index sheet for the county in OS/1/7. Once you have identified the area on the index map you will see some large squares on the index sheet with a number in the middle – this is the number of the six-inch sheet. So if the the sheet number you require is 6 and 7 of County Antrim then the PRONI reference number will be OS/1/1/6 and OS/1/1/7.

Follow the same system for the revised six-inch maps, which provide more details (field boundaries et cetera) than the first edition, except that the classification is OS/6. The townland of Dunrevan in County Tyrone would be OS/1/6/6/16.

OS/7 is the classification for Irish Grid maps for the 1950s onwards.

OS/8 is the classification for 163 towns in Northern Ireland which were printed.

OS/9 complements OS/8: this a collection of older manuscript town plans. For the index to the borough of Belfast consult the wall map in the Public Search Room.

A copy of the Conventional Signs used on the six-inch maps of the Ordnance Survey can be found at the end of OS/2.

A *Union List of Belfast Maps to 1900* was published in 1998 by the Local History Panel of the Library Information Services Council (Northern Ireland) and can be consulted in the Public Search Room.

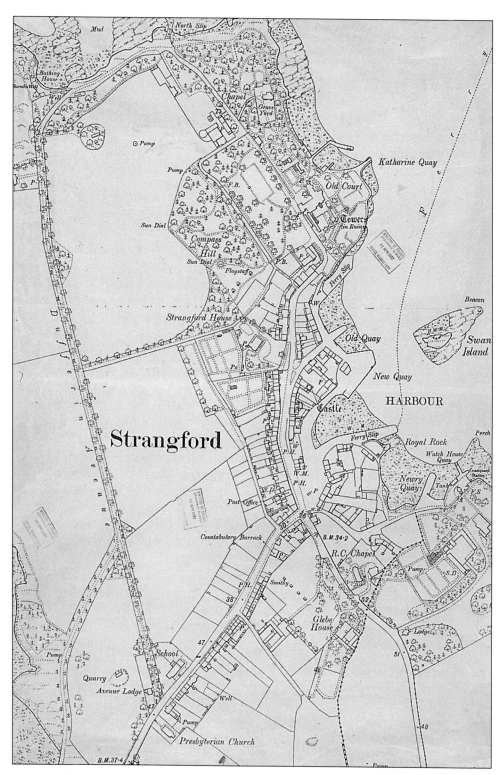

Ordnance Survey town plan of Strangford, County Down, 1900
(scale: 1/1056)

OS/8/157/1

This list covers both manuscript and printed maps up to 1900 held by the Belfast Education and Library Board at Belfast Central Library, by the Linen Hall Library, by the National Museums and Galleries of Northern Ireland/Ulster Museum and by the Public Record Office of Northern Ireland. It excludes Ordnance Survey maps and plans and those maps which do not depict a discernible street plan. From the 1820s onwards the most comprehensive maps have been produced by the Ordnance Survey, but other maps continued to be produced for specific purposes and these could contain additional information useful to the local historian.

The maps are listed in chronological order, each entry containing:

- a description of the map
- the scale, where given, which is represented as a statement as well as a fraction
- the size in centimetres to assist in ordering photocopies if possible or permissible
- details of various versions where known
- the location of the map

EXAMPLES

1625–6

'A Booke of survey of lands belonging to ye Right Honourable ye Lord Viscount Claneboy' by Thomas Raven. Eighteen 'plots' and a subsidiary title page are devoted to the 'territories of east and west Holywood', including Ballymacarret, Ballyhackamore, Knocknagoney and Dundonald.

> Scale: 30 Scottish perches to an inch (1:6,750)
> Size: atlas measuring 36 x 49
> Originals held by North Down Borough Council   T/870/1

1832

'A New and Correct Plan of the Town of Belfast with all the Improvements, Streets, Squares, Docks & Bridges . . .' [by James Kennedy].

> Scale: not given
> Size: 39x49
>   45x53 (in UM)
>   48x42 (in PRONI)
> Engraved by J. Thomson
> PRONI [T/1541/10]; LHL [Belfast 26 and 26A]; UM [463–1912]

Guides to maps and plans *c.* 1570–*c.* 1830 for each Northern Ireland county have been bound together in one maroon-coloured volume, entitled *Maps–Plans* (refer to the plan of the Public Search Room, page 2). The free PRONI leaflet, *Local History 8: Ordnance Survey Maps*, can be obtained in the Public Search Room

ORDNANCE SURVEY MEMOIRS

A remarkably detailed and unique source for the history of the northern half of Ireland on the eve of the Famine are memoirs intended to accompany the first edition of the six-inch Ordnance Survey maps. Taking up suggestions made by some of his officers, Thomas Colby sent an instruction to the master general of the Ordnance in 1826 that 'a great variety of material towards the formation of statistical and other reports will be collected whilst the work is in progress' and that this was to be recorded in remark books. Colby's deputy, Sir Thomas Larcom, set about implementing this order with an enthusiasm which eventually alarmed the government. In 1837 the first volume, that for Templemore parish, County Londonderry, was published; since it cost £1,700 to produce, this was also the last to be printed. When the directive to cease work on the memoirs came in 1840 all of Ulster had been covered and a small number of parishes further south had been completed: thus local historians in the north can use the memoirs to help them understand a period when population pressure on the land was at its most acute.

The memoirs cover each parish, subdivided into townlands, and provide information on natural features, natural history, geology, towns, public buildings, 'gentlemen's seats', manufactures, mills, roads, canals, railways, the history of the parish, ancient monuments, scenery, local government, dispensaries, relief of the poor, 'habits of the people', and the economy. Comments on habits and customs are particularly revealing – indicating, for example, the local impact of the evangelical revival and the Catholic renewal – and their frankness may have weighed with the authorities when it came to deciding whether or not to continue with the project.

Fortunately the memoirs have been published by the Institute of Irish Studies at Queen's University Belfast, edited by Angelique Day and Patrick McWilliams. The memoirs for the six Northern Ireland counties, and for Cavan, Donegal, Monaghan, Queen's County (now Laois), Roscommon, Sligo and Tipperary can be consulted on microfilm at PRONI, reference number MIC/6: these contain some material not included in the published volumes, notably on the origin and meaning of townland names. Typed extracts are available in T/2383, which include copies of topographical drawings.

The original memoirs can be found in the Royal Irish Academy, Dublin; the National Archives in Dublin have reports on Londonderry parishes and Ordnance Survey correspondence; the Ordnance Survey in Dublin has the Field Name Books by John O'Donovan; and the National Library of Ireland holds the Larcom Papers.

EXAMPLES OF EXTRACTS FROM THE ORDNANCE SURVEY MEMOIRS

The degeneracy in the breed of cattle throughout this parish and the whole of the surrounding district is reduced to the lowest possible degree. Nothing can be more inferior than the general class of horses and horned cattle exhibited in the fairs. Pigs are the only animals in which any concern appears to have been taken in their breeding. The low Dutch breed of short-legged, short-eared and small-headed pig are most esteemed and have supplanted in very great degree the long-shanked and hideous-looking animals formerly so common . . .

PARISH OF DRUNG, COUNTY CAVAN

The wretched hovels, scantily covered with straw, surrounded and almost entombed with mire, which everywhere present themselves throughout the parish, sufficiently testify that the total absence of all activity in industry is one source of the wretchedness and misery which almost overwhelms the land . . .

PARISH OF CURRIN, COUNTY MONAGHAN

Their wakes, which formerly had been scenes of amusement, are now observed with decorum and propriety, the evening being spent in reading aloud the Scriptures. During the night refreshments, consisting of bread and cheese, whiskey, pipe and tobacco, are handed about . . .

Their dialect, particularly in the more remote parts of the parish, is strongly Scottish, as are also their idioms and old saws, which are very quaint and pithy, and plainly indicate their extraction . . .

PARISH OF DONEGORE, COUNTY ANTRIM

It is customary as soon as the children of a family grow up for them to marry, usually at an early age, and begin the work on their own account, building mud huts wherever a few acres of land are to be obtained, and struggling through life in poverty and wretchedness, but apparently contented and cheerful . . .

PARISH OF AGHALURCHER, COUNTY FERMANAGH

The inhabitants of all sexes and classes are perhaps a more immoral race than is to be found in any other rural district in Antrim. Their drunkenness and intemperence is everywhere proverbial . . . What makes their immorality the more disgusting is the openness and want of shame with which it is exhibited. The women whenever from home, or indeed whenever they can procure the means, drink raw spirits in such quantities as would astonish any but a native . . . the number of sudden, violent and premature deaths among them, solely from the effects of intemperence, is appalling . . . Some have fallen off carts or staggered into a hole on the way home. Others have been smothered, 2 have committed suicide, several have lost their reason . . .

PARISH OF ISLANDMAGEE, COUNTY ANTRIM

The free PRONI guide leaflet, *Local History 3: Ordnance Survey Memoirs*, can be obtained in the Public Search Room.

FURTHER READING

Aalen, F.H.A., Kevin Whelan and Matthew Stout, eds. *Atlas of the Irish Rural Landscape*, Cork, 1997

Andrews, J.H. *History in the Ordnance Map*, Dublin, 1974
—— *A Paper Landscape*, Oxford, 1975

Hamilton, Gertrude. A catalogue of large-scale town plans prepared by the Ordnance Survey and deposited in PRONI: *Northern Ireland Town Plans, 1828–1966*, PRONI, 1981

Parkhill. Trevor. 'OS Maps in the Public Record Office of Northern Ireland', *Ulster Local Studies*, vol. 14, no. 2, winter 1992

Lease from the Right Honourable Sir Gustavus Hume to John Dickson, Creave, County Donegal, and Alexander Patterson, Tully, County Fermanagh, 2 October 1724

4
LANDED ESTATES RECORDS

'Land is life,' the radical Fintan Lalor declared in the middle of the nineteenth century. This statement was true for the vast majority of people in Ireland at the time, even in Ulster where the industrial revolution had made most progress. As late as 1821 only 8 per cent of the inhabitants of the northern province lived in towns.

In medieval times great estates were held from the English Crown by descendants of Norman conquerors, including the earldom of Ulster by the de Burgos, Desmond by the FitzGeralds, Ormonde by the Butlers and Meath by the de Lacys. Extensive parts of Ireland remained under the control of Gaelic lords, particularly in Ulster west of the River Bann. Areas most thoroughly colonised lay outside Ulster and today contain many placenames with the suffix *-town* or *-ton* and the prefixes *castle*, *court*, *grange* and *grove* (such as Trimleston, Courtown,

Grangegorman and Castleroche). The contrast between the anglicised Pale and Gaelic south Ulster is particularly striking in the Armagh–Louth borderlands. In the fourteenth and fifteenth centuries the native Irish overran much territory which had been part of the Irish lordship – most of the earldom of Ulster fell to the Clandeboye O'Neills, for example. However, during the Tudor period, as the power of the English Crown recovered, some Gaelic lords accepted English titles under the 'surrender and regrant' scheme, including Conn Bacach O'Neill who became the first Earl of Tyrone.

The conquest of Ireland was completed at the start of the reign of James I and Ulster was 'planted' with British colonists – this area included much of Antrim, Down and Monaghan, counties not included in the official scheme. Further rebellions, wars, penal legislation and upheavals led to additional confiscations and redistributions: the end result was that most of Ireland was divided into great estates, a state of affairs which prevailed until the beginning of the twentieth century. On an island where urban development outside of Dublin was slow, the great majority of the Irish were living on the land as leaseholders, 'tenants at will' (tenants without leases, often working land sublet by leaseholders), 'cottiers' (those renting small farms or potato gardens from year to year, usually paying rent either in kind or by unpaid labour), and agricultural labourers. The estate owners were descendants of Norman conquerors (such as the FitzGeralds, earls of Kildare), descendants of Gaelic lords who had avoided dispossession (such as Lord O'Neill of Shane's Castle and the MacDonnells, earls of Antrim), descendants of those granted estates in the seventeenth century, or those who had purchased lands from these grantees (such as the Stewarts of Mountstewart in the Ards peninsula).

As many of the estates were large, the owners exercised extraordinary power, most obviously in Ulster where estates were transformed into manors by the granting of royal patents. The landlord class monopolised membership of both Houses of the Irish parliament; controlled local government either through grand juries in the counties or as owners in the boroughs – Belfast, for example, was ruled by a sovereign and twelve members of the corporation all chosen by Lord Donegall, who also selected both MPs for this borough; and possessed rights and privileges over estates and tenants specified in patents from the Crown, including the right to hold manorial courts.

PRONI holds a remarkable collection of landed estates records, not only for the six counties of Northern Ireland but also for Monaghan, Donegal and Cavan, and some material from elsewhere on the island, notably the King-Harman, Gore-Booth and Kenmare papers. This is the result of work by senior staff in going out to persuade owners to deposit their papers. The records include rentals, account books, leases, maps, surveys, wages books, lists of tenants, valuations and correspondence. Some of these holdings are of use to those seeking to link local history with national, international and diplomatic history, including those of the Londonderry estates (for Robert Stewart, Lord Castlereagh), and of the Macartney estates (for Sir George Macartney). The principal value, however, is to local historians. Those interested in researching the history of towns in Ulster may not be fully aware, for example, that landed estates records are very informative, especially for those towns which were not incorporated. The Adair papers are useful for Ballymena, the Southwell papers for Downpatrick, the Abercorn papers for Strabane, the Stewart papers for Cookstown and the Downshire papers for Hillsborough.

Where do you begin? The very quantity of documentation can in many instances be extremely intimidating – the Kenmare papers, for example, weigh one and a half *tons!* Fortunately, help is available within the Public Search Room.

The *Valuation Books* (refer to the plan of the Public Search Room, page 2) for 1860, also known as 'Griffith's Valuation', provide you with the landlord's name for a specific area. Obviously this applies to that date, or just before 1860, but estates (with varying shapes and fortunes) often remained in the possession of one family from the early seventeenth century to the beginning of the twentieth century. In Griffith's Valuation the landlord's name appears under 'immediate lessor'.

The *Guide to Landed Estates Records*, in two volumes (refer to the plan of the Public Search Room). This is set out alphabetically by county, with estate names entered alphabetically within each county, together with descriptions of the records and reference numbers.

The *Personal Names Index* can provide reference numbers for landlords' names. Remember that there are many records of all kinds for persons with the name 'Robert Stewart' and there is more than one Clotworthy Skeffington.

Deputy Keeper's Reports and *Statutory Reports* let you know of recent acquisitions. The most significant new records are described and analysed in some detail by an expert and can not only save the researcher a great deal of time but also highlight features which few would expect to find.

The **D** *calendars*, colour-coded blue in the Public Search Room, contain typescript introductions to the most important landed estates records. It is difficult to exaggerate how valuable these are to the local historian if the estate described is in the area you are researching. The history of some estates has been written, for example the studies of the Donegall and Downshire estates by W.A. Maguire, but others are confined to unpublished doctoral theses or have yet to be researched (see page 33 for further reading lists). These introductions, therefore, provide easy-to-read histories of leading families and their estates which may be impossible to obtain elsewhere.

Both the **T** *calendars*, colour-coded red, and the **D** *calendars* in the Public Search Room contain extensive extracts from the correspondence of landlords, agents and tenants. These give clear indications whether or not it is worth ordering out a document and may even provide you with enough information without going further.

ESTATE RECORDS TEND TO FALL INTO THE FOLLOWING CATEGORIES

Rent rolls, which list tenants, townland by townland, and specify rents in money or in kind, and record obligations such as fencing, ditching, house building and military service in times of danger.

Leases are much more detailed than rent rolls. A lease, which is a legal agreement between the owner and tenant, not only gives the name of the tenant but also those of some of his children, often with their ages. In the eighteenth century, and often in the nineteenth century, leases in Ulster were usually granted for 'three lives', that is the lease expired when all three people named in the lease had died. Naturally, tenants liked to name those who seemed likely to live the longest and leaseholders who named George III when he was Prince of Wales were particularly fortunate because he was eighty-two when he died in 1820. As the population rose and profits from the land increased, some estate owners preferred to shorten leases to provide more frequent opportunities to raise the rent. For example, the 2nd Marquess of Downshire replaced leases for three lives and thirty-one years with leases for one life and twenty-one years. Where Lord Downshire felt a tenant had a farm which was too small to be profitable, he refused to renew the lease – a policy directly opposite to that of his mother, the Dowager 1st Marquess, who was keen to create as many tenants as possible to increase the number of voters she could control. A problem with many landowners was that some of those named in leases emigrated overseas with no news of their whereabouts or whether or not they were still alive. The Penal Laws made it illegal to give a Catholic a lease longer than thirty-one years until 1782. In practice few Protestants were able to obtain leases of longer duration.

EXAMPLE OF EXTRACT FROM LANDED ESTATES RECORDS

Lease of a tenement in Antrim issued by Sir Hugh Clotworthie (D/207/14/3)

> This indenture is made the twentieth daye of January 1625, Between
> Sir Hugh Clotworthie of Antrim in the Countie of Antrim knight
> and the lady Mary his wyfe of the one partie, and William mcKinlaye
> of Antrim aforesayd husbandman and Katherin his wyfe of the other
> partie . . . doe demise graunt and to farme lett vnto the sayd William
> mcKinlaye and Katherin his wyfe, all that tenement garden and
> backsyd, scytueat lyinge beinge in the towne of Antrim aforesayd, and
> on the south syde of the high streete there . . . YEALDEINGE and
> payeing vnto sayd Sir Hughe Clotworthie the lady Marie and the
> heires of the sayd Sir Hughe for the before demised premisses the
> yerely rent of ten shillings currant and lawful mony of and in England
> halfe yerely to be payd att midsomer and Christmas, by even and
> equall portions, alsoe payeinge yerely twoe good fatt capones att
> Christemas twoe good fatt hennes att Shrovetyde, twoe good fatt
> duckes at Lamas, and twoe good dayes wourkes yerely to be performed
> in the tyme of harvest or when they shalbe demaunded, by the body
> of an able man or men . . .

Rent ledgers show the tenants' names, and when and how they paid
their rent. Rents were collected twice a year, the half year falling due
on the 'gale days' of 1 May and 1 November. The custom in Ireland was
to allow six months' credit, a practice known as the 'hanging gale' –
much criticised in the Land War because indebted tenants were at the
mercy of their creditor landlords. Rent ledgers contain the names of
'tenants-at-will', those who rented land without the formal arrangement of a lease – indeed the majority of farmers fell into this category
until land purchase legislation at the beginning of the twentieth century made many of them freeholders. A substantial number of tenants,
however, sublet land from leaseholders and do not therefore appear in
rent ledgers, the poorest of them being referred to as cottiers.

Eviction was not as easy as is sometimes thought. When rents were
not forthcoming, landlords tried exhortation but then had to go to
court to begin ejectment proceedings. Ejectment proceedings were
almost always employed to enforce payment rather than to get the tenant out. The power of landlords, however, was only very slightly limited until William Gladstone's Land Act of 1881 and in the 1860s and
1870s John George Adair and Lord Leitrim were able with impunity to

throw tenants who had paid their rent off their estates in County Donegal. Evictions were most frequent during periods of crisis, such as the Famine and immediately after, and the late 1870s and early 1880s when continuous wet weather in Ireland coincided with a fall in agricultural prices resulting from cheap American meat and grain imports.

Wages books record the names and earnings of estate labourers, household servants and gardeners. Agricultural labourers in the nineteenth century always outnumbered tenants of all kinds on the land and yet they attracted far less attention in parliament and in the press – not to speak subsequently from historians. Labourers found employment from landlords on their demesnes (parts of their estates which they did not let out but farmed directly), freeholders, leaseholders and even, at times, from tenants-at-will.

Maps made for landowners are discussed in Chapter 3. Not only do they plot tenants' holdings but they can provide highly informative detail on how estates were farmed, on settlement patterns, changes in farming practice, the reduction in woodlands, the impact of new roads, drainage schemes, et cetera.

Land agents' notebooks can be of great assistance to the researcher seeking to build up a picture of rural life in a particular locality.

Correspondence from agents, landlords and tenants can also be very useful to the local historian. For example, the Downshire papers in PRONI not only contain a thousand volumes of accounts but also thirty thousand letters, most of which are concerned with the day-to-day management of the estates during the first half of the nineteenth century.

EXAMPLES OF EXTRACTS FROM LANDED ESTATES CORRESPONDENCE

Lord Annesley acted as the Marquess of Downshire's agent. In 1815 one tenant, William Reilly, challenged the positioning of the 'mearing' or boundaries of his farm; Annesley advised Downshire not to be 'hurried into any Decision when there could be the least doubt in your Mind. It being a Year since Mr Reilly was in Suspicion of my Maps, without produceing any document indicating against their Accuracy, I did consider he had admitted it . . .' The dispute dragged on for a couple of years and on 3 July 1817 Annesley wrote again to Downshire on the matter (D/671/C/33A/21):

My Dear Lord,

I had by last Nights post the honor of your Lordships letter of the 20th mentioning the directions You had given Mr William Reilly;

who called on Me, was shewn the Act of Parliament I referred to, and
under which a Mearing may be settled without any Interference of
any legal Person, or Expence what ever, except that of making the
Mearing which must be very inconsiderable . . .

Earlier in the year Annesley was deeply concerned about the impact of
a bad harvest the previous year – appalling weather had, in fact,
destroyed crops across the United Kingdom. On 21 February 1817 he
wrote to Downshire (D/671/C/33A/16):

My Dear Lord,

The wretched situation of the poor of the parish of Kilmegan, from
the price of provisions, is such that the worst Consiquence is much to
be dreaded. Provisions are now at a heighth that is beyond the power
of many families to purchase them, they are increasing weekly, it is
dreaded that many poor families will neither be able to purchase
them; or seed to sow or plant for the ensuing Crops; and I am
requested to apply to your Lordship for advice and assistance; so that
some steps may be taken to alleviate their present situation, and
provide for next season. A Monthly Contribution has been considered
most expedient, with an Advance for the purchase of seed Oates and
Potatoes . . .

Downshire was keen to increase the financial yield from his extensive
estates but he was clearly moved by his agent's letter (D/671/C/33A/17):

Hillsborough
22nd February 1817

. . . I shall have great pleasure in cooperating with your Lordship in
the laudable object you have in view for the relief of the distressed in
our respective Estates, which I believe comprize the whole parish.
  I perfectly concur with you as for the expediency of purchasing seed
Oats and Potatoes for the next Crop, & I shall direct Mr.Lyne to pay
particular attention to this subject, both as to the best mode of
obtaining an early supply the ensuing season, and to enable my
Tenants to be punctual in the payment of their Rent, which is the
first consequence both to themselves and their Landlord . . . Mr Lyne
will take my directions to inscribe in my name such a Sum, as upon
consulting with your Lordship may be deemed right . . .

Militia, yeomanry and muster records are often to be found in estate papers for the seventeenth, eighteenth and early nineteenth centuries: these list men liable for service in various defence forces.

Valuations are available in many estate collections and generally contain the names of tenants.

The return of owners of land: the government ordered the compilation of a list of all the landowners of Ireland, a task carried out between 1871 and 1876, and published under the title *Return of Owners of Land of One Acre and Upwards, in the Several Counties, Counties of Cities, and Counties of Towns in Ireland* to which is added *A Summary for Each Province and for All of Ireland (Presented to both Houses of Parliament by Command of Her Majesty)*. This provides an extremely useful snapshot of landownership shortly before the break-up of great estates under land purchase legislation. The names of 32,614 owners (including those with leases of ninety-nine or more years, and those with leases with the right of perpetual renewal) are listed alphabetically by province and county together with the extent of their lands, the valuation and their addresses. Another 36,114, not named, owned property of less than one acre. This return was reprinted in 1988 by the Genealogical Publishing Company Inc., Baltimore, with the title *Return of Owners of Land in Ireland 1876*. The return was drawn upon by several writers and publishers, including activists in the Land League: the best known is U.H. Hussey Burgh's *Landowners of Ireland 1878* which lists landowners with five hundred acres or more, or those with land valued at £500 or more.

Encumbered estates records: lists of landowners and their estates mask the complexity of legal arrangements which often made ownership less outright than it appeared in returns. For example, an owner might have mortgaged all or part of his estates; lands or income might have been set aside for the upkeep of a dowager during her lifetime; and other entail arrangements which may have been made. Some owners, such as the 2nd Marquess of Donegall, were hopelessly in debt: his son, the 3rd Marquess, inherited debts of close on £400,000 – *fourteen* times the annual rental – in 1844. Though none died of starvation, many landlords were ruined financially by the Great Famine. As a result the government put through the Encumbered Estates legislation in 1848–9 to speed up the sale of estates overburdened with debt. An Encumbered Estates' Court (which became the Landed Estates' Court in 1853) gave out the proceeds of sales to creditors and gave clear titles to new owners. The hope was that enterprising entrepreneurs from Britain would invest in Irish property and raise levels of prosperity and economic activity, but most of the speculators were Irish landowners, such as the notorious John George Adair who bought the Derryveagh estate in

County Donegal and played his part in helping to precipitate the Land War.

The eighty-three volumes of Irish Encumbered Estates Rentals in PRONI cover the whole country; they are divided into counties, town-lands or houses, and tenements. Not only do they name owners, creditors and purchasers, but also rentals, tenants' names, maps and (sometimes) surveys. An index to the Encumbered Estates' Courts can be consulted in the Public Search Room.

THE BREAK-UP OF THE GREAT LANDED ESTATES

Between 1849 and 1857, about three thousand estates totalling 5 million acres (around a quarter of the land area of Ireland) were sold under the terms of the encumbered estates legislation. However, tenants felt increasingly that little had been done to protect their rights. The 'Ulster tenant right', by which a tenant could be compensated for improvements and could sell his interest in a farm to an incoming tenant, had no standing in law and was challenged, for example, on the Downshire estates and set aside in dramatic fashion by John George Adair and Lord Leitrim.

Falling prices due to cheap imports from overseas and successive seasons of bad weather led to a sharp increase in evictions for non-payment of rent and an eruption of rural unrest known as the Land War. In addition to 'coercion', the government produced a Land Act in 1881 which made the Ulster Custom legally binding across the country and set up a Land Court to arbitrate on rents. As the nineteenth century drew to a close the Conservative administrations turned to land purchase as a solution: the government would act as a bank to lend money to tenants to buy out their landlords. It was not until 1903 that legislation, the Wyndham Land Act, was produced, attracting a majority of tenants to buy. Legislation by Liberal governments on the eve of the First World War compelled landlords to sell and the outcome was that the great estates melted away to be replaced by family-owned farms – a social revolution, largely bloodless, almost without parallel in the rest of Europe.

Land Acts generated a prodigious output of records, mostly produced by the Irish Land Commission (which succeeded the Land Court): these are kept in the Land Registry Archive. Arranged by county, these records provide valuable insights on conditions on the land, farming practices, and give full details on holdings on each estate with their boundaries. PRONI has the archive relating to the six counties of Northern Ireland: this is arranged alphabetically for each county by estate or owner. The first part of the PRONI reference number of each document is LR/1; the number of the Land Commission box follows next; and the last digit of the reference number is required because each box may contain some documents relating to other estates.

EXAMPLE

DATE	NAME	COUNTIES	BOX NO.	RECORD NO.
1746–1931	Beresford-Ash, Col. W. LR1/1343/3/A–C	Londonderry/ Tyrone	1343	NI 01491

It is often forgotten that when the Church of Ireland was disestablished in 1869, it was the greatest landlord in Ireland. This property had been looked after by the Ecclesiastical Commissioners; between 1870 and 1881 it was the responsibility of the Commissioners of Church Temporalities in Ireland; and from 1881 the property was transferred to the Irish Land Commission.

The free PRONI guide leaflet, *Local History 9: The Commissioners of Church Temporalities in Ireland* (FIN/10/10), can be obtained in the Public Search Room.

FURTHER READING

Crawford, W.H. 'Landlord-tenant relations in Ulster, 1609–1820', *Irish Economic and Social History*, II (1975), pp. 5–21

Dowling, Martin W. *Tenant Right and Agrarian Society in Ulster 1600–1870*, Dublin, 1999

Hewitt, Esther, ed. *Lord Shannon's Letters to His Son*, Belfast, 1992

Maguire, W.A. *The Downshire Estates in Ireland, 1801–45*, Oxford, 1972
—— *Living Like a Lord: The Second Marquis of Donegall 1769–1844*, Belfast, 1984

Vaughan, W.E. *Landlords and Tenants in Ireland 1848–1904*, Dundalk, 1984
——*Landlords and Tenants in Mid-Victorian Ireland, 1848–1904*, Oxford, 1994

Tithe Valuation of the Parish of Drumbo

Page from the tithe valuation of the parish of Drumbo, County Down, featuring the townland of Carryduff, 1829

FIN/5A/118/B
(page 21)

5
TITHE RECORDS

The tithe system, which nominally earmarked one-tenth of the produce of the land for the upkeep of the clergy, was introduced into Ireland with English law which, in medieval times, operated only in those areas controlled by the Crown. In Gaelic society lands granted by local kings and lords were set aside for the maintenance of the Church. The Tudor conquest and the Jacobean plantations led to the confiscation of monastic and Church lands: most were granted to royal favourites but some were assigned to the Established Church, for example, fertile estates in north-east Donegal to the Bishop of Derry. Tithes, however, formed the main source of income for the Anglican Church and were vested in the Crown which often granted or sold them to laymen – the tithes of Comber parish, for example, became the property of Lord Londonderry and those of Shankill parish were acquired by Lord Donegall.

The majority of the people on the island (never less than three-quarters of the population) remained Catholic and, in addition, a high proportion of Protestants in Ulster were Presbyterians who did not conform to the Established Church. The tithe was therefore widely regarded as an unjust impost, even more so after the unrepresentative Irish parliament abolished the tithe on grazing land, which favoured large landowners over smallholders who concentrated on tillage. Property owners, Church of Ireland clergy, and tithe proctors (men employed to collect the tithe) often became hated figures in the Irish countryside.

Symptoms of unrest became so frequent by the beginning of the nineteenth century that the Westminster government was forced to take remedial action. The tithe was a tax on the produce of the land and was usually levied in kind in the form of corn, eggs, poultry, butter, et cetera. which made its levying highly visible. The 1823 Tithe Applotment Act set up a procedure for 'commutating' payment in kind into payment in cash. The valuation was based on the productive capacity of the land, which in turn was worked out by reference to the average price of corn over the seven years prior to 1 November 1821. In 1832 the Commons Select Committee on Tithes praised the act as leading to 'a moderate assessment on the land' but the seven years chosen were years of high prices resulting in high valuations and, in addition, tithes were now imposed on pasture land. In Ulster the impost averaged about 4 per cent of the rental.

A 'tithe war' erupted in Leinster in the 1830s and at the same time violent incidents were frequent in Ulster leading, for example, to the death of one man at Keady, County Armagh, in December 1834. Further legislation in 1832 made commutation on the basis of the valuation procedure compulsory and in 1838 the Tithe Rent Charge Act reduced tithe payments by a quarter and absorbed them into the ordinary rents payable to the landlords. This took some of the heat out of the situation but it was not until William Gladstone disestablished the state Church (effective from 1 January 1871) that the tithe disappeared from the Irish scene.

The tithe records are especially useful to the local historian researching the decades prior to the Great Famine. The whole of Ireland was valued, parish by parish, the results being recorded in tithe applotment books compiled between 1823 and 1837. Each volume deals with a single parish, the content being subdivided by townland. Recorded against each townland were the names of occupiers, the areas subject to tithe, the valuation and the tithe payable. The investigator is given an invaluable picture of the Irish countryside when it was densely populated and approaching the crisis of the Famine, which includes descriptions of the quality of the land, differentiating between arable and pasture, and a record of the names of those who made use of it – this last is of particular use to the genealogist as the population censuses of 1821 and 1831 were largely destroyed in the Four Courts fire of 1922. Placenames are often spelled differently from those adopted by the Ordnance Survey and this needs to be remembered by those using the Topographical Index. Not all parishes and townlands are covered, as some were too unproductive to have tithe levied on them and some were tithe-free for other reasons.

The PRONI Guide to Tithe Records (1994) lists townlands, giving their parish and county locations, the date of valuation and the PRONI reference number. Townlands which cannot be reconciled to townlands in the Topographical Index of Ireland are printed in italic. For example:

TOWNLAND	PARISH	COUNTY	YEAR	PRONI REF. NO.
Ballynahatty	Drumbo	Down	1829	FIN /5/118 p. 5

Remember that townland names can appear more than once:

Ballynahatty	Drumragh	Tyrone	1830	FIN /5/126 p. 2

And, for example, for the six counties of Northern Ireland there are five townlands named Legacurry.

The PRONI guide leaflet, Local History 9: The Commissioners of Church Temporalities in Ireland (FIN/10/10), can be obtained in the Public Search Room.

6
CHURCH RECORDS

A loss most keenly felt after the destruction of the Four Courts in Dublin in 1922 was that of the Church of Ireland registers. This was because between the sixteenth-century Tudor conquest and Church reformation, and the disestablishment of 1871, the Church of Ireland was the state Church and recorded baptisms, marriages and burials of Catholics, Protestant dissenters and others who were not members of the Established Church. The Parochial Records (Ireland) Act of 1875 declared baptism and burial registers prior to 1871, and marriage registers prior to 1845, to be public records which should be deposited in the Public Record Office of Ireland. The records of 1,006 parishes had been deposited by 1922 but of those only 4 escaped destruction. Local historians have therefore to depend heavily on other surviving sources. In compensation there are numerous published histories of Christian denominations and of individual churches, parishes and congregations; and in 1994 PRONI produced, with the University of Ulster and the Ulster Historical Foundation, the *Guide to Church Records*, revised in 1997, which is of great assistance to the local historian and genealogist.

The parish was an ecclesiastical division of less significance than in other parts of western Europe where the town was more important as an economic and social institution. Following Church reforms in the twelfth century and the extension of English rule, the parish became an administrative unit. When the whole island had been conquered, and the Church of Ireland became established in fact as well as in law, the civil parishes and the Church of Ireland parishes were identical. Later, urban growth and the amalgamation of some parishes and dioceses in the nineteenth century meant that civil parishes increasingly had different boundaries from those of the Church of Ireland.

As the Catholic Church emerged from the penal era new parishes were created and others altered in shape – in short, Catholic parishes bore little relation to civil parishes and so searching under several parishes is usually necessary to find all the records relating to one Catholic parish. Presbyterians, Methodists, Baptists and other

Page from a marriage register for the Church of Ireland
parish of Kilkeel, diocese of Dromore, 1859–96   CR/1/15/B/3

Protestant sects did not have a parish structure.

Begin by consulting the *Guide to Church Records*, which is a binder-volume to be found in the Public Search Room. This is organised by civil parish and within each the churches are arranged alphabetically by denomination. The abbreviations used for denominations are:

B. – Baptist   C. – Congregational
C.I. – Church of Ireland   M. – Methodist
MOR. – Moravian   N.S.P. – Non-Subscribing Presbyterian
P. – Presbyterian   R.C. – Catholic
R.P. – Reformed Presbyterian   R.S.F. – Religious Society of Friends.

EXAMPLE: CLONDUFF, COUNTY DOWN

C.I.   Clonduff (Down diocese)
        Baptisms 1782–1871; marriages, 1786–1850; burials, 1787–1849
        and 1864–73; accounts, 1871–1913; vestry minutes 1811–70
                                        (MIC/583/2, 30, 31)

        Vestry minutes, 1870– ; churchwardens' accounts, 1811–1903
                                        (in local custody)

BAPTISMS.

(The Year 18   )   Page

N°.

Charles H Scott of *Robert & Alice Scott*
was Born *fourth* and Christened *5th March 1818*
Registered *5th March 1818* by me *Luciad Waring Rector*

Isabella Mathers Daugr of Samuel & Jane Mathers
was Born *17th April* and Christened *19th April 1818*
Registered *19th April 1818* by me *Luciad Waring Rector*

Margret Wright Daugr of John & Mary Wright
was Born *12th April 1818* and Christened *19th April 1818*
Registered *19th April 1818* by me *Luciad Waring Rector*

Page showing baptismal entries for the year 1818 in the Church
of Ireland register for the parish of Kilkeel, diocese of Dromore   CR/1/15A/1

- P. Clonduff
  Baptisms, 1842–1968; marriages, 1864–1914 (MIC/1P/126)

- P. Hilltown
  Baptisms, 1845–1968; marriages, 1864–1914 (MIC/1P/127)

- R.C. Clonduff (Dromore diocese)
  Baptisms, 1850–80; marriages, 1850–80; funerals, 1850–81
  (MIC/ID/29)

  Printed history of Clonduff parish from the seventeenth century
  to 1940 (CR/2/4)

In the *Guide to Church Records* no attempt is made to locate churches
in Belfast within a civil parish since most of Belfast fell within one
parish (Shankill) – these churches are listed under 'Belfast'.

Pre-1870 Church of Ireland registers survive for about two hundred
parishes in Northern Ireland and these have been copied by PRONI.
Few Catholic or Presbyterian registers survive for the period before
1800. All surviving Presbyterian registers have been copied by PRONI
and microfilm copies of Catholic parish registers, from about 1830 to
1880, for the historic nine-county province of Ulster are held at PRONI.

Church records are most frequently consulted by genealogists but they are of central importance also to the local historian. The church for long was the hub of the community and, until recently, church attendance figures in Ulster were the highest in Europe and, in some cases, amongst the highest in the world. Over most of Ulster, sectarian feeling was strong from the early seventeenth century onwards and, especially in rural areas, people gave their loyalty to their co-religionists and their Church before they gave it to their locality. Church records often illustrate national events and demonstrate how these impacted at parish or townland level. For example, documentary evidence on the terrible Irish famine of 1740–1 is extremely sparse but burial records from some surviving Church of Ireland registers graphically show the fearsome rise in deaths in many areas. The parish register for Magheralin, County Down, indicates a grim harvest at the beginning of 1742:

FEB 1   Buried Matthew son of John Lavery of Drumnaferry
1   Buried Susanna Wife of James Macoun of Edenballycoggill
4   Buried Murthagh Heany from Kilwardlin
6   Married David Bell and Margaret Parker of Ballym"mean
10   Buried Mary Dau: of Edward and Susanna Hoyle of Magheralin
13   Buried a Child of John Jenkins of Maralin Shoemaker
14   Buried a Child of Bryan Lavery's from Moyrah Parish
17   Buried Elizabeth Dau: of Widow Conky of Maralin
18   Buried Mary Dau: of Bryan McIlboy of Drumnaferry
19   Buried Elinor Dau: of Widow McClatchy of Maralin
19   Buried Richard Dempsy of Maralin
19   Buried Hugh Dalos of Dromore
19   Buried Edmund Lavery from Ballinderry
20   Buried Jean Dau: of Thomas & Catherine Walker of Dromo & Dromore
22   Buried Margaret Wife of Knocker Lavery of Edenmore
23   Buried Jean Dau: of High Walker of Tullyard
23   Buried Margaret Read a poor Woman from the Glebe
24   Buried Andrew Son of Dan: & Mary Campbell of Dromo & Dromore
25   Buried Patrick Son of Patrick McKeonan of Lissmean

The Great Famine of the 1840s is far more extensively documented: a good deal of evidence for localities comes from church records for all denominations and from vestry minutes and correspondence of priests, ministers and clergy.

The following is an entry in the parish register of Ballinascreen in County Londonderry, made by the Church of Ireland rector, the

Reverend Samuel Montgomery:

> On the three last days of July and the first six days of August 1846 the
> potatoes were suddenly attacked, when in their full growth, with a
> sudden blight. The tops were first observed to wither and then, on
> looking to the roots, the tubers were found hastening to
> Decomposition. The entire crop that in the Month of July appeared so
> luxuriant, about the 15th of August manifested only blackened and
> withered stems. The whole atmosphere in the Month of September
> was tainted with the odour of the decaying potatoes.
>   Increase the fruits of the earth by Thy heavenly benediction.

CHURCH OF IRELAND RECORDS

Despite the destruction of the Public Record Office in Dublin in 1922,
records of sixty-five parishes in Northern Ireland going back to 1800
survive. The *28th Report of the Deputy Keeper of the Records in Ireland,
1896* lists all parishes in alphabetical order and identifies those parishes which did not send their records to the PRO and thus avoided
destruction in 1922.

   In addition, certain types of Church of Ireland records were not handed in for public keeping. The most important of these are vestry minutes, which contain a great deal of information useful to the local
historian, including: baptism, marriage and burial entries going back to
the seventeenth century; names of church wardens, cess applotters, cess
payers, names of the confirmed and names of overseers of the roads and
of the poor; and details on widows, orphans and other destitute people
receiving relief. Other locally-held church records include confirma-
tion registers, account books, registers of vestry men, and – occasionally – censuses of parishes, such as Christ Church in Belfast in 1852.

   PRONI has copied surviving records covering the pre-1871 baptisms
and burials, pre-1845 marriages and early vestry minute books for
churches in Northern Ireland. All the pre-1900 records for churches in
counties Donegal, Cavan and Monaghan have been placed on microfilm. Original records and paper copies can be found under the PRONI
reference code CR/1; other paper copies under T/679; and the microfilm
copies under MIC/1. The PRONI *Guide to Church Records* identifies
Church of Ireland records available only in the Library of the
Representative Church Body, Dublin.

For example, extracts from the registers of the Church of Ireland cathedral of St Columb's, Derry, seem at first to be no more than the recording of baptisms, marriages and deaths. A closer look reveals a fearsome rise in deaths as a result of appalling harvests, severe weather conditions, hunger and fever epidemics during the spring of 1718–19 (the year then still began in April, like our own financial year): in March a total of twenty-six were buried, seven children were baptised and one couple was married.

Church of Ireland records recently microfilmed include: marriage registers of Killead parish, County Antrim, 1845–1997 (MIC/1/293); baptismal, marriage and burial registers of Ballymore parish, County Armagh, 1846–1923 (MIC/1/324); and vestry minute books and baptismal, marriage and burial registers of Drumcree parish, County Armagh, 1767–1906 – the vestry minute books not only give the parish accounts and details of parochial business but also contain lists of 'Protestants' and 'Romans', poor in receipt of aid from the parish between 1765 and 1827 (MIC/1/21/2). The original Preachers' Books of Muckamore parish, County Antrim, 1824–1975 (CR/1/75) remark on how bad weather had an adverse impact on church attendances.

The PRONI guide leaflet, *Local History 2: Church of Ireland Vestry Records*, can be obtained in the Public Search Room.

METHODIST CHURCH RECORDS

John Wesley visited Ireland on many occasions and his followers were won principally from the Established Church. The formal break with the Church of Ireland came in stages and baptisms, for example, were mostly recorded in the Church of Ireland until about 1830. There were splits in the Methodist congregations, the Primitive Wesleyan Methodists breaking away in 1816 and not reuniting until 1878 (Primitive Methodists retained links with the Church of Ireland and did not have their own baptismal registers until the 1860s). The Methodist New Connexion distanced itself from the Church of Ireland and reunited with the Irish Methodist Conference in 1905. Of particular interest to the local historian are membership registers or quarterly class rolls (some go back as far as 1819), circuit schedule books and administrative records classified under MIC/429/1. These show the relative strength of Methodism in different localities, the progress of the temperance movement, emigration, et cetera.

The Methodist unit is the circuit, not the parish, and the composition of circuits changed periodically. At the beginning of MIC/1E there is an alphabetical index to all circuits and Methodist churches. The Cavan, Monaghan and Donegal records have been copied by PRONI and are to be found under the reference codes MIC/1E and CR/6. The administrative records of the Methodist Conference chart the various changes in the district to which the circuits belonged and changes within the circuits themselves (CR/6/3).

In 1999 PRONI acquired thirty-nine volumes of records of the Monaghan, Aughnacloy and Castleblayney circuits (CR/6/15, CR/6/16, CR/6/17) which give a thorough survey of Methodism in the area between 1823 and 1975. The deaths section of the earliest register concerning the joint Monaghan and Aughnacloy circuit contains detailed written portraits of members, including records of their conversion experiences. Other papers in this archive provide information on temperance organisations, Sunday Schools, numbers of members and attendants, membership registers and accounts.

PRESBYTERIAN CHURCH RECORDS

Presbyterians in Ireland were never completely united in one church organisation. Presbyterianism arrived in Ulster from Scotland during the Plantation in the seventeenth century and was poorly represented outside the province, except amongst the radical woollen weavers of the Coombe in Dublin. In the eighteenth century divisions amongst Presbyterians largely reflected those in Scotland. Seceders and Covenanters tended to be conservative, strict and ascetic, but the main bone of contention was the Westminster Confession – a seventeenth-century catalogue of doctrine – which was accepted by Old Light but rejected by New Light Presbyterians, who believed that interpretation of the Scriptures was best left to individuals. Recent research has shown that Presbyterian participants in the rebellion of 1798 were drawn from all divisions and were by no means exclusively New Light Presbyterians. Presbyterians living west of the River Bann were, with a few and notable exceptions, opposed to the United Irishmen and many joined the yeomanry and the Orange Order.

Towns sometimes had (and have) more than one Presbyterian Church and these were, and are, referred to by number, 1st, 2nd, and so forth. These usually reflected population growth but often it was not the need for more accommodation but doctrinal disputes that led to the setting up of new congregations. For example, congregations broke away from the Synod of Ulster (founded in 1733) because they objected to the use of patronage in appointing ministers and sought a more evangelical approach, and became known as Seceders. In Belfast in the closing decades of the eighteenth century the 1st, 2nd and 3rd Presbyterian churches were beside each other in one street, Rosemary Lane: doctrinal differences between them were small and all three took a liberal stand in politics. In Saintfield, County Down, the 2nd congregation was formed because some Presbyterians there objected to the support given to the United Irishmen by the Reverend Thomas Ledlie Birch, minister of what became the 1st Saintfield Presbyterian Church.

Following a long and well-chronicled dispute between conservatives led by the Reverend Dr Henry Cooke, and the liberals led by the Reverend Dr Henry Montgomery, most Presbyterians sided with Cooke and united in the Synod of Ulster and also in the Presbyterian Church of Ireland in 1840. A relatively small number of liberals remained aloof to form the Non-Subscribing Presbyterian Church. The Free Presbyterian Church has no connection with the 'Wee Frees' of Scotland (journalists occasionally make this error) and is an evangelical church formed by the Reverend Ian Paisley in 1951.

Presbyterians, along with other Protestant dissenters, were subject to restrictions imposed under the Penal Laws, though they were not as severe or as comprehensive as those placed on Catholics. Until 1782, for example, Presbyterians had to marry in Church of Ireland churches and it was only from 1845 that Presbyterian ministers could legally marry a Presbyterian and an Anglican. This means that many Presbyterian baptisms, marriages and burials are to be found in registers of the Church of Ireland. However, Presbyterian churches were not legally compelled to place their records in the Public Record Office (now the National Archives) in Dublin and therefore avoided the destruction of 1922.

Some registers go back to the eighteenth century. Burial registers are rare because there were few Presbyterian cemeteries. Of particular value to the local historian are the session and committee minutes. These not only provide records of baptisms and marriages, but record new recruits, and evidence of emigration, disputes and transgressions. There are few censuses of congregation. Presbyterian records copied by PRONI can be found under the reference codes MIC/1P and CR/3; the catalogues for these have alphabetical indexes to the churches. Some records, not copied in PRONI, are held by the Presbyterian Historical Society, Belfast.

EXAMPLE OF EXTRACT FROM CHURCH RECORDS

> Aghadowey Session Book 1702–61 (Presbyterian Historical
> Society)page 37 Session 24 August 1704:

> Jo. Boid [states] he saw John Wooden one morning lying in bed with
> Margt Finla. But the wife of said John Wooden was sitting by the bed.
> Jo. Boid being confronted, John Woodend denied of ever he was in
> bed naked with the said Margt Finla but ownes ye another servant
> maid one Galt lay betwixt his wife and ye wall at another time. Jo.
> Boid takes a voluntary oath ye John Wooden was in naked bed with
> Margt Finlay and he saw him rising and putting on his cloths. They
> being removed from the session after pondering the case judged that
> John Wooden is free of the sin of adultery with Margt Finla but the
> session thinks he was in bed with her tho out of no ill design but
> inadvertently his wife leaving them in bed together and herself sitting
> by the bed. The session judges Jo. Wooden being in bed with Finla
> was unseeming and offensive and agreed to give him a sessional
> rebuke. He was rebuked and exhorted to mutuel forgiveness and
> friendship which was accordingly agreed.

Was this a fuss over nothing? Or is this an early-eighteenth-century
instance of an Ulster *ménage à trois*? In the end, since it was one man's
word against another and the women seem to have stuck by their man,
the elders compromised with a sessional rebuke.

RECORDS OF THE CATHOLIC CHURCH

Manuscripts and other surviving archives of the Church in Ireland
before the Reformation are preserved in Trinity College Dublin,
libraries in Oxford and London, and repositories in old universities and
ecclesiastical centres on the Continent such as Rome, Salamanca,
Louvain, Paris and Milan. Henry VIII made himself head of the Church
in Ireland as well as in England, and from the reign of Edward VI, with
the exception of that of Mary, this 'established' (Anglican) Church was
Protestant. The Act of Union in 1801 united the Established Churches
of Ireland and England until William Gladstone disestablished the Irish
Church in 1869 (effective from 1871).

   The Catholic Church was on the defensive, therefore, from the middle of the sixteenth century onwards. The period of most severe

persecution was 1649–60, during the Commonwealth, when Catholic worship was illegal. This was followed by greater toleration during the Restoration but the defeat of the Jacobites in 1691 resulted in the Penal Laws, imposed between 1695 and 1726. The aim of this penal code was not to extirpate Catholicism but to negate the political and economic power of the Old English and Gaelic landed classes which had remained with the Catholic Church. Catholic bishops and monks were exiled; but priests could remain and Catholics could still worship provided priests did not wear vestments in public, churches did not have bells and steeples, pilgrimages were not held and Catholics did not teach in schools. In practice the religious clauses proved difficult to enforce – pilgrimages to Lough Derg in County Donegal continued, for example – but the legislation virtually removed the Catholic gentry especially in Ulster (the leading Catholic family conformed to the Established Church in the eighteenth century). The Catholic Church in Ireland recovered rapidly from the middle of the eighteenth century but it was comparatively poorly organised in Ulster until the Catholic renewal got under way from the 1850s onwards. The result is that local records of Catholic churches and parishes are overwhelmingly confined to the nineteenth and twentieth centuries.

Catholic registers, mostly dating from the 1820s, are almost entirely for baptisms and marriages, with names of sponsors and witnesses included. Some entries are written in Latin. Since a Catholic parish can often be made up of parts of two or more civil parishes it may be necessary to search under several parishes: cross-references are made in the *Guide to Church Records*. Most Catholic parishes have more than one church and sometimes each church kept its own register. PRONI has microfilm of all the pre-1880 registers for the nine counties of Ulster, to be found under the reference code MIC/1D.

OTHER PROTESTANT DENOMINATIONS

THE RELIGIOUS SOCIETY OF FRIENDS (QUAKERS)

Quakers first appear in Ireland in the middle of the seventeenth century and from the outset they were meticulous in the keeping of records. Not only did they keep registers of births, marriages and burials but also documents recording offences (such as marrying outside the Society) and sufferings arising from religious beliefs (such as punishment for refusal to pay tithes). PRONI has copies of all the records of the Lisburn

Meeting House, which include Lurgan, Richhill, Ballyhagen, Grange, Antrim and Cootehill, found under the reference code MIC/16.

NON-SUBSCRIBING PRESBYTERIANS

Those Presbyterians in Ulster who refused to subscribe to the Westminster Confession formed the Presbytery of Antrim in 1725. In the 1820s Non-Subscribers were forced out of the Synod of Ulster and the break was complete by 1840. Some Non-Subscribing records are Presbyterian; the earliest and one of the most interesting is the session minute book for Templepatrick, 1646–1743, PRONI reference number MIC/1B and CR/4.

COVENANTERS

These were Presbyterians who adhered strictly to the Scottish Covenants of 1638 and 1642, and who set up the Irish Reformed Presbytery in 1763. By 1800 there were twenty-eight congregations but – unlike the Non-Subscribers – they were admitted to the Synod of Ulster. Their copied records are to be found under the reference code MIC/1C or CR/5.

CONGREGATIONALISTS

This denomination only developed in Ireland in the nineteenth century from the setting up of the Irish Evangelical Society in 1814. The records, to be found under the reference code CR/7, are primarily baptism and marriage registers, and minute books. For additional records relating to the Irish Evangelical Society see CR/7/2 add.

BAPTISTS

The first Baptists appeared in Ireland in the seventeenth century but the denomination really only established itself on the island in the nineteenth century. The earliest records begin in the 1860s and consist of marriages and minute books (which record adult baptisms). The records have not been copied at PRONI but are held by the Baptist Union of Ireland in Belfast.

MORAVIANS

This denomination was brought from the Austrian empire to Ireland by John Cennick in 1746 and soon had societies in the counties of Antrim, Down, Armagh, Londonderry, Cavan, Monaghan, and Dublin. Their records were kept meticulously and include registers of baptisms, marriages and burials, membership registers and ministers' diaries. The copied records, from originals held in Gracehill Moravian Church, are found under the PRONI reference code MIC/1F. The *Church Book of the Moravian Brethren Congregation at Cootehill* has been microfilmed for PRONI: this records baptisms, marriages and burials for the years 1765 to 1917 and not only lists members but also gives details on people's former religious denominations, date of reception into this County Cavan congregation, marital status and burial site (MIC/1F/5). Registers for the congregation at Kilkeel, County Down, provide information on baptisms, marriages and burials for 1834–1919 (MIC/1F/6).

Photograph showing an Armagh municipal technical school commercial D/2886/A/1/4/60
class at work, *c.* 1913 (from the photographic and business records of the Allison
Photographic Studio, Armagh, *c.* 1895–*c.* 1950)

7
EDUCATION RECORDS

PRONI holds records for schools from the seventeenth century
onwards and most of the early ones are for institutions set up in the
wake of the Elizabethan and Jacobean conquests and subsequent confiscations and plantations. Parliament authorised the setting up of a free
grammar school in every diocese in 1570 but progress on these diocesan
schools was slow until the following century.

The Plantation of Ulster included an order that a free grammar
school should be established in each of the six confiscated counties, in
the words of the 1608 Order in Council, 'to stir up and recall the
province of Ulster from superstition, rebellion, calamity and poverty to
the true religion of Christ, and to obedience, strength and prosperity'.

EARLY RECORDS INCLUDE

> Return of lands granted to schools in Ulster, dated 1615 and signed by Lord Deputy Sir Arthur Chichester (DIO/4/8/1)

> Papers relating to the free or royal schools at Dungannon, Armagh and Enniskillen, 1615 (DIO/4/2–4)

> Papers of the Armagh Diocesan Registry concerned with the running of the royal schools, 1615–1900. These also include records of the founding and administration of the Erasmus Smith schools set up in the eighteenth century, endowed by the state, which aimed to convert Catholic children to Protestantism through education. A copy of Charles II's charter, 26 March 1670, provides explanations and specifications 'to teach twenty poor children from within a radius of two miles' is included (reference for the charter is DIO/4/8/9/1/1).

Many landowners set up schools from the 1830s onwards. Together with the royal schools, these endowed, charitable and private schools raised Ulster above the other three provinces in terms of educational provision.

EXAMPLES OF EIGHTEENTH- AND EARLY-NINETEENTH-CENTURY RECORDS INCLUDE

> Correspondence, title deeds, minute books, et cetera, relating to the 'blue-coat' Southwell Charity School, Downpatrick, 1722–1970 (D/2961)

> Records of the Lurgan Free School, set up by the Brownlow family in 1783 to educate children of Lord Lurgan's tenants, regardless of religion, in Shankill parish, 1786–1854 (D/499)

> Report of the schools in Ballymoney parish, County Antrim, by the Reverend Robert Park. It includes a full report on Ballymoney Free School founded in 1806 (D/499)

> Records of the Thomas Jamison Charity School, Annahilt, County Down (D/3693)

All these records come from Protestant schools, or schools managed by Protestants for both Protestants and Catholics. The Penal Laws, enacted from 1695 to 1726, prevented Catholics from having their own schools and together with other restrictions, made it illegal for

Catholics to educate their sons abroad or to take degrees at Trinity College Dublin. Some of these proved difficult to enforce and, in any case, most of these disabilities had been removed by 1793, but it took time to set up Catholic schools (Daniel O'Connell, the man who led the movement for Catholic emancipation, was educated in France, for example) and access to education was largely through Protestant schools.

Catholics who did not want to send their children to Protestant schools (particularly the proselytising schools set up by the London Hibernian Society) were prepared to pay to send them to 'hedge schools', so called because they were often held in the open during the summer months and payment was frequently made in kind in the form of food, turf and whiskey. A famous description of a hedge school is given in tales written just before the Great Famine by William Carleton, a Tyrone convert from Catholicism to Protestantism. By the early nineteenth century these hedge schools, no longer illegal, were referred to as 'pay schools'. A high proportion of these were in Ulster (in 1824, teaching 125,272 pupils out of a total of 157,184). There were a large number of schools at this stage but many were in poor condition and provided only the most rudimentary tuition. In the wake of the evangelical revival schools were being established to convert Catholics to Protestantism and this was a potential cause of friction.

The Act of Union notwithstanding, Ireland was not governed as if it was simply a region attached to England and Wales. The government tended to be more experimental and interventionist in Ireland: the island, for example, was the first part of the United Kingdom to have a national police force and a medical dispensary service. Ireland was also the first part of the UK to have a national state-sponsored system of elementary education.

By 1827 the Commission of Irish Education Inquiry had produced no fewer than twenty-three reports and finally, in 1831, the chief secretary, E.G. Stanley (later Lord Derby) founded the system of national education. The schools were to be non-denominational, with clergy excluded from teaching posts: this produced a storm of protests from Presbyterians, Catholics and Anglicans. In practice the schools became denominational, with churches providing sites and managers, and the commissioners paying for buildings and teachers' salaries. Managers, often appointed by either Catholic or Church of Ireland bishops, exercised a near-dictatorial power over their schools and made sure that only teachers of their own denomination were appointed.

Around 2,500 National Schools were created in Ulster between 1832

Date of Entrance.	Register Number.	PUPIL'S NAME IN FULL.	Date of Pupil's Birth.	Religious Denomination as stated by Parent or Guardian.	RESIDENCE.	Position or Occupation of Parent or Guardian.	State the Name and County of the last National School at which the Pupil attended ; and the Class in which there enrolled.		
							School.	County.	Class.
15th May 1923	656	1 Lavery Mary Margt	6/16	R.C.	Quoniamstown	Labourer	Never at school before		
29th May 1923	657	2 Dagens Elizabeth	6/17	R.C.	Scollogstown	Orphan	"	"	"
4th June 1923	658	3 Grimes Maimie	11/18	R.C.	Whiggamstown	Labourer	"	"	"
10th Apr. 1924	659	4 Byrne Bridie	8/16	R.C.	Coniamstown	Farmer	"	"	"
5th May ...	660	5 Rooney Bridget	8/19	R.C.	Grangecam	Labourer	"	"	"

Name of Pupil.	School Year ending.	No. of Attendances made in the Year.	Class in which Enrolled.	Precise Date of Admission to that Class.	Class in which Examined.	RESULTS OF EXAMINATION HELD BY TEACHER. (Maximum mark in each subject is 10.)										Total School Fees paid in school year if any.	If Pupil's Name be struck off Roll, give date.	If Pupil be re-admitted, give date.	Destination of Pupil.
						Reading, etc.	Writing and Composition.	Arithmetic.	Drawing.	Grammar.	Geography.	History.	Needlework.	Vocal Music.	El. Science.	Other Branches.	£ d.			
1 Lavery Mary Margt	30·6·23	26	Inft	15·5·23																
	30·6·24	103	"	"	Inft															
	30·6·25	127	"	"	"															
	30·6·26	154	I	1·7·26	Inft															
	30·6·27	128	II	1·7·27	I										Prom.					
	30·6·28	117	III	1·7·28	II	7	3	0	6						—					29·6·29
	30·6·29	128	—	1·7·28	III	3	2	0	2	0	2		0	4	Prom.					
Dagens Elizabeth	30·6·23	10	Inft	29·5·23															30·6·31	
	30·6·24	134	"	"	—															
	30·6·25	137	"	"	Inft															
	30·6·26	160	I	1·7·26	Inft															
	30·6·27	176	II	1·7·27	I										Prom.					
	30·6·28	155	III	1·7·28	II	9	9	8	8						—				6·1	
	30·6·29	170	IV	1·7·29	III	8	7	6	5	3	6		7	5	R_m					
	30·6·30	174	I	1·7·30	IV	9	8	10	4	7	9		8	6						

Page from the register of girls, Leggamaddy National School,
County Down, 1919–46

and 1870. In PRONI, the grant-aid applications are classified under ED/1: these yield a great deal of information on, for example, the names of teachers, dimensions and conditions of schoolhouses, numbers of pupils and daily average attendance. Some national schools were attached to workhouses and supervised by boards of guardians, while others developed out of estate schools (for example, those set up by the Drapers' Company in County Londonderry [D/3632], which came under the control of the National Education Board around 1874, and those under the patronage of the earls of Antrim [D/2977]). Despite the many criticisms levied at the national schools, illiteracy rates fell sharply: in 1841, 53 per cent of Irish persons of five years upwards could neither read nor write but by 1914 this figure had fallen to 14 per cent.

The PRONI guide leaflet, *Local History 5: National School Records*, can be obtained in the Public Search Room.

PRIVATE SCHOOLS

Private education did not develop to the same extent in Ireland as it did in Britain, partly because of the close associations between rural communities and church institutions, and partly because in the nineteenth century the Irish gentry and aristocracy increasingly sent their sons (and less frequently their daughters) to public schools in Britain (which, despite their name, were and are private). Some churches ran private schools, including the 1st Holywood Presbyterian Church which had as one of its pupils James Craig, later Northern Ireland's first prime minister. Others became prestigious secondary schools which eventually were drawn partly into the state system as grammar schools in the twentieth century. Belfast Academy was founded in 1786 because the merchant and professional families in the rapidly growing town were dissatisfied at the inadequate provision made by Lord Donegall. It later moved from Academy Street to the Cliftonville Road and in 1885 became Belfast Royal Academy. The Royal Belfast Academical Institution was founded in 1810 by liberal Presbyterians (including Dr William Drennan, the real founder of the Society of United Irishmen in 1791) as an Ulster equivalent of Scottish colleges where so many of them had completed their education. Meanwhile Catholics were establishing their own private schools: St Malachy's College in Belfast and St Columb's in Derry were set up initially with the intention of preparing young men for the priesthood as seminarians before going on to Maynooth College. Those colleges, along with girls' schools such as St Dominic's in Belfast, and Christian Brothers schools, were to become part-funded by the state in the twentieth century – the levels of funding and the degree of state control were matters of vigorous debate and contention, particularly as the Education Acts of 1922, 1930 and 1947 were being drafted and implemented. The records of these institutions mostly remain on the premises but several schools and colleges have had comprehensive histories written about them.

THIRD-LEVEL EDUCATION

For the Protestant upper classes Trinity College Dublin, founded in 1592, was the university to which they sent their sons: those wishing to acquire legal qualifications generally only went to London after graduation. Catholics were excluded until 1793 and, regarding the college as an Ascendancy bastion, avoided it until the late twentieth century. Presbyterians, too, were prevented from taking degrees there by the requirement to subscribe to the Oath of Supremacy and throughout the eighteenth century they obtained university education at Scottish institutions, then amongst the most radical and educationally advanced in western Europe.

After restrictions on Catholics receiving education abroad had been lifted, the French Revolution and the Napoleonic Wars made travel to overseas seminaries difficult. In 1795 Maynooth College was founded, with government funding, to give Catholics a seminary at home. The Royal Belfast Academical Institution not only provided secondary education but also established degree courses which made travel to Scotland unnecessary for those Presbyterians aspiring to join the professions. A college to train Presbyterian ministers was built in Derry in 1852 and opened in 1865. It became one of five institutions making up the Royal University until 1909 when the national University was founded; the Presbyterian college, known as Magee Presbyterian College, preferred instead to be connected to Trinity College. In 1970 it was integrated with the New University of Ulster and is today a campus of the University of Ulster.

EXAMPLES OF DOCUMENTS RELATING TO THIRD-LEVEL EDUCATION

Some 2,500 volumes, files and documents of the Magee Presbyterian Trust, 1850–1984, are held in the PRONI reference number (MPT/)

Correspondence, 1762–70, from William Mussenden discussing the expulsion of his son from Trinity College, clearly because the authorities disapproved of his unitarian views (D/354/1062):

The having any doubt about the doctrine of the Trinity is understood by them as calling into question the truth of Christianity . . . that a young gentleman of nineteen could however be supposed to have any settled opinions upon this point and that he should be called on by account of inquisitors to answer such absurd questions as were then put him is really astonishing, what could an inquisition do more unless to inflict pains and penaltys which I thank God is not in their power.

Correspondence, 1799–1841, on the history and development of Maynooth College (DIO/(RC)/1)

About seven hundred volumes, files and documents comprising records of the New University of Ulster (later the University of Ulster) at Coleraine and Magee University College, 1845–1970.

A considerable controversy raged over the siting of the new university at Coleraine in the 1960s, and nationalists and unionists in Londonderry city combined to protest against the failure to locate it in their city (NUU/)

Correspondence, memoranda, reports, speeches, et cetera, relating to the university issue (D/2511)

Manuscript memoirs of Dr Florence Stewart, a general practitioner in north Belfast between 1937 and 1970. She writes of her days as a medical student at Queen's University, Belfast, 1927–33 (D/3612/3/1)

MODEL SCHOOLS

Model schools were set up in 1846 as part of the training system for teachers. In each district model school, selected trainees were supervised in their teaching of pupils over six months. Because they were administered directly by the Commissioners for National Education, the schools were denounced by the Catholic hierarchy and as a result the number of schools set up was limited. Detailed records survive for some Ulster model schools, notably in Newtownards, Enniskillen and Belfast.

EXAMPLES OF DOCUMENTS RELATING TO MODEL SCHOOLS

Records of Ballymoney Model School, 1856–96 (SCH/12)

Records of Lurgan Model School, 1863–1945 (SCH/482)

A description of occupation by troops and the Royal Irish Constabulary of Belfast Male Model School during the riots of August 1886. In September the medical attendant, Dr McConnell, complained that 'the occupation of the school-house and the premises by the military must be injurious to the health of the pupils and teachers'. (ED/8/1/30)

AGRICULTURAL SCHOOLS AND REFORMATORY
AND INDUSTRIAL SCHOOLS

From 1833 onwards some national schools were designated agricultural schools which aimed to teach theoretical and practical rudiments of farming. In 1870 the Powis Commission recommended the closure of most of these and by 1896 only forty-seven national schools had farms attached. In Ulster the three most important were Greenmount, County Antrim, Enniskillen, and Loughry, County Tyrone. The PRONI policy file for Northern Ireland agricultural colleges, 1958–69, is AG/16

The National Education Board designated some schools as industrial in which only two hours a day were to be set aside for academic work. The Reformatory Schools Act of 1868 turned these schools into institutions for juvenile offenders. Eight of these schools were in Northern Ireland in 1921, reduced to seven in 1929 – four for girls and three for boys. A file in PRONI, 1869–1958, deposited by the ministry of home affairs with administrative detail and inspectors' reports, includes the following report in 1901:

> His face may be clean, but his ears and neck accuse him of neglecting them at his morning ablution . . . when you look at his boots you are puzzled, for he has a left one on each foot . . . his feet are neither sweet-looking nor sweet-smelling; he is lazy and selfish . . .

NURSERY SCHOOLS

After a hesitant start in the 1920s, nursery schools got government funding to make more female labour available during and after the Second World War. In 1950 most existing nursery centres were transferred to local education authorities. Minute books of education authorities and ministry of education 'N' Nursery files, 1929–61, include the following:

Minute books of County Armagh Education Committee 1925–73
(LA/2/7AC)

Department of Education nursery files, 1929–68 (ED/24)

Minute book of the management committee of Downpatrick Nursery School, 1951–5 (SCH/703)

Papers of Roberta Hewitt in the Hewitt papers (D/3838)

LOCAL AND CENTRAL GOVERNMENT PAPERS ON EDUCATION

The role of local government in education was increased by legislation in 1898–9 and, in Northern Ireland, in 1922, 1930 and 1947 in particular. The suspension of devolved government in 1972 returned control to central government and to – largely government-appointed – education and library boards. The activities of all these central and local bodies are well represented in PRONI and include:

Records of the Belfast County Borough Council Education Committee, 1894–1961 (LA/7/7)

Policy files of the six Northern Ireland County Education Committees and those of Belfast, Londonderry and Bangor (ED/16)

Records of the education and library boards, including school management committee and sub-committee minutes, annual reports and schemes of management (AELB/)

GOVERNMENT PAPERS INCLUDE

Printed parliamentary papers – including reports and examination papers – from 1834 to 1951 (ED/10)

Microfilm of government memoranda encompassing 162 volumes between 1880 and 1916 (MIC/216)

Primary schools files (ED/9)

Technical schools files (ED/4)

Ministry of Education policy files (ED/13)

Ministry of Education Private Office records including sensitive/ contentious material on religious instruction (ED/32)

Parliamentary questions on education, Northern Ireland, 1922–67
(ED/30)

Papers of the Lockwood Committee on Higher Education which controversially recommended the location of Northern Ireland's second university at Coleraine (ED/39 and FIN/58)

Nine reports of the Registrar General's Office containing an analysis of the 1981 census of Northern Ireland in relation to education
(RGO/8)

EDUCATIONALISTS

The papers of two highly influential educationalists held at PRONI are of particular interest:

The papers of Vere Foster, inventor and publisher of the immensely popular copy books, a generous philanthropist and founder of the Irish National Teachers' Organisation (D/3618)

The educational papers of Thomas O'Hagan, twice lord chancellor of Ireland (1868–74 and 1880–1), and commissioner of national education (1858–85). A Catholic, educated at the Royal Belfast Academical Institution, he strove to persuade his county-religionists to make the most of the educational opportunities increasingly made available, particularly by the Royal University. (D/2777)

8
POOR LAW RECORDS

There was no state provision for the poor in Ireland at all until 1838 and relief was given only by private benefactors and charities. For example, Clifton House in Belfast was built in 1762 on land given by Lord Donegall and funded by the Belfast Charitable Society. In 1834 the parish-based system of relief in England which had operated since Elizabethan times was replaced by the highly controversial New Poor Law. Despite many recommendations to the contrary, this new legislation was applied to Ireland four years later with minor modifications only. Inspired by Malthusian fears of a population explosion of the destitute, the government was determined to make relief as unattractive as possible lest the poor become dependent on hand-outs and breed recklessly. Ireland was divided into 137 'unions' (civil parishes united to form a Poor Law administrative area), 27 of which were in the six counties of what is now Northern Ireland.

Relief could only be given within a workhouse: conditions there were to be 'less eligible', that is less attractive, than the worst prevailing outside; inmates had to work; children were separated from their parents; and husbands and wives could not share the same quarters. The buildings were hardly finished when the island was swept by potato blight engulfing Ireland in the Great Famine between 1845 and 1852. The workhouses were overwhelmed – indeed over much of the country the system all but broke down – and there was some (rather uneven) relaxation of the rule that relief could only be given within the workhouse. 'Outdoor' relief became more accepted later in the nineteenth century and the workhouses increasingly became the last refuges of orphans, the elderly, families of men who were imprisoned, unmarried pregnant girls and other destitute persons. The shadow of the workhouse remained longer in Northern Ireland than in the rest of the United Kingdom, where it was removed in stages in the 1920s and 1930s; it disappeared only in 1948–9 with the introduction of the National Health Service.

For details of the records which have survived for each union, consult the grey calendars on the shelves on the left-hand side of the Public Search Room. The twenty-seven unions are listed in alphabetical order,

RETURN of PAUPERS who were Admitted into, or Discharged from, the Workhouse; and of the number of Sick, and the number Born, or who Died therein, during the Week ended SATURDAY,—— 6th day of February 1847.

	ADMITTED.							DISCHARGED.						DIED.					
	Males, aged 15 and upw^{ds}.	Fe-males, aged 15 and upw^{ds}.	Boys under 15.	Girls under 15.	Chil-dren under 2.	BORN. Males.	BORN. Fe-males.	TOTAL	Males, aged 15 and upw^{ds}.	Fe-males, aged 15 and upw^{ds}.	Boys under 15.	Girls under 15.	Chil-dren under 2.	TOTAL	Males, aged 15 and upw^{ds}.	Fe-males, aged 15 and upw^{ds}.	Boys under 15.	Girls under 15.	Chil-dren under 2.	TOTAL
During the Week ended as above,	2	7	5	7	1			22	12	17	9	12	1	51	14	17	24	29	11	95
Remaining on the previous Saturday, as per last Return,	152	283	223	193	42			893												
TOTAL,	154	290	228	200	43			915												
Deduct Discharged and Died during the Week ending as above,	26	34	33	41	12			146												
REMAINING ON THE ABOVE DATE,	128	256	195	159	31			769												

RETURN OF SICK AND LUNATIC PAUPERS.

	No. of Paupers in Hospital on the above date.	No. of Lunatics and Idiots in Workhouse on the above date.	OBSERVATIONS In case of any unusual number of these classes of Paupers.
		In sepa-rate Wards. / In Wards with other Inmates.	
In Work-house,	218		
In Fever Hospital,	59	· / 14	
Total,	277	Total, 14	

Number of Inmates that the Workhouse is calculated to contain, 800 ___ + 48 in Fever Hospital.

NEXT MEETING of Guardians to be held on Thursday, the 11 day of February 1847.

COPY of MINUTES of Proceedings of the Board of Guardians, at a Meeting held on Thursday, the 11 day of February 1847.

PRESENT: In the Chair, Lord Lurgan

Other Guardians: Colonel Blacker, Mess. Greer,
Cuppage McCartan Ruddell Reilly
Hatland Atkinson, Ballick, Hyde,
Dolling, Hanny, Waddell, Douglass,
Henry and Turtle ___

The Minutes of last Meeting were read and Signed.
The Register Book was produced, examined, and authenticated, from No. 5575
to No. 5594 both inclusive, by the signature of the Chairman, and counter-
signature of the Clerk.
The Clerk's Report on the execution of Orders previously made by the Board
was read, to the following effect:

That he has attended generally to all
Orders on the last Minutes ___

The Master is ill in Fever, the School
Master to take his place ___

for example, BG/1 for Antrim, BG/7 for Belfast, and BG/24 for Newry. BG/28 – Gortin, County Tyrone – was united with Omagh in c. 1870.

Most Poor Law records are closed for a hundred years from the latest date in each volume; this is because documents include information about individuals, the disclosure of which would cause distress or danger to living persons or their descendants. However, enough records remain open to assist the local historian: for example, minute books – available for all the unions – are very revealing for the outdoor relief unrest in Belfast in 1932. The board of guardian records are key sources for investigating the impact of the Great Famine on different localities. Below are examples from the minutes of the Irvinestown (then known as Lowtherstown) union (BG/15/A/4) for the spring of 1849 when the Famine was officially declared to be over:

> Gentlemen . . . I happened to go to the Dormitories when the Paupers were going to bed, and anything more disgusting than the scene I witnessed could not be imagined, buckets are left in the middle of the floor some of them leaking, to these the Paupers have recourse in all their wants, and the effluvia arising from it is insufferable. I am informed they do not go further than their bedside . . .
>   signed, Henry D'Arcy, Guardian
>   3rd January 1849

Poor Law Commissioners were concerned that some unions made women break stone which they considered unsuitable labour for females. A letter was sent to the Lowtherstown guardians and they replied as follows on 10 March 1849:

> Gentlemen, In reply to your letter of the 6th Inst, referring to the manner in which Women are employed in this Workhouse, I am desired to state that the only reason given by the Commissioners in their letter to the Guardians, of the North Dublin Union against the employment of Women in Stonebreaking vizt that it is contrary to common usage does not apply in this district or any of this portion of the North of Ireland, and that the Guardians are all aware that that species of employment is thankfully received and eagerly sought for by many females in this Country . . . therefore the Guardians would be slow by casting a slur on that species of employment to mar the honest efforts of persons wishing to be industrious and self relying . . .

Though about a million people died during the Famine the island was remarkably peaceful and in 1848, the Year of Revolutions on the Continent, the only violent incident of note was the 'Battle of Widow McCormack's Cabbage Patch' in County Tipperary. The Lowtherstown Union – a particularly badly run Union in the view of the commissioners – witnessed some mildly disorderly scenes in 1849:

> Week ending Saturday 14 April 1849:
>
> The Master Reported that on Sunday morning last the Women
> broke 23 panes of glass in their dayroom and were otherwise very
> insubordinate –
> Ordered that all Milk be stopped until Next Board Day.
> Ordered – that no fire be allowed in the women's day room in
> consequence of the paupers having attempted to burn the house . . .

For all its shortcomings, the Poor Law did introduce genuine representative institutions into the Irish countryside: until 1898 counties were governed by grand juries made up of local landlords and property owners. Boards of guardians, however, were elected from the outset by the ratepayers and the opportunity was given to people of comparatively humble origin to participate in public life. As in most representative bodies, tempers could become frayed, as is revealed in this minute from the Lowtherstown board:

> The following Notice of Motion was given by H.W. Barton, Esqre,
> vizt
>
> Sir, Take Notice the Next Meeting of this Board I attend, I will
> propose that whenever one Guardian calls another a 'liar' the
> Chairman do call him to Order.
>
> signed H.W. Barton, 23rd May 1849

In fact, Barton appears to have let the matter drop and did not attend meetings for some time after that date.

Complete sets of minutes exist for almost all the unions and these form a valuable resource for local historians for the period 1838 to 1948. Other records include admission and discharge registers (which provide details such as names, age, marital status, occupation and why relief needed to be given), outdoor relief registers, registers of births and deaths, and punishment books. The printed valuation books (known as 'Griffith's Valuation') are organised on the basis of Poor Law unions.

Crowds gathered outside Crumlin Road Courthouse during elections for Belfast Corporation, 1894

D/3905/E/2

9
LOCAL GOVERNMENT RECORDS

In medieval times a sure sign of the establishment of English royal power in a locality in Ireland was the appointment of a sheriff to rule over a county, and his ability to call out a posse of the county to pursue lawbreakers indicated whether or not that power was firmly rooted. On the troubled margins of the Irish lordship, Ulster did not experience the rule of the sheriff in this period, not even in the earldom of Ulster east of the River Bann where the seneschal, representing the Crown, had his work cut out maintaining any sort of authority. The extension of Tudor control in the sixteenth century changed everything in the north: the introduction of a sheriff in Fermanagh helped to precipitate the Nine Years War in 1594 which ended in the complete conquest of Ulster by 1603 and the imposition of the authority of the sheriff at county level.

In the seventeenth century local government made a clear distinction between incorporated towns and counties. Incorporated towns were those granted the right to have a corporation, that is a body with limited powers of self-government and the right to send one or two members to the Irish parliament. Nearly all these towns were 'close' boroughs in which the local landlord decided almost everything: in Belfast, for example, the 'lord of the castle' (Lord Donegall) chose the 'sovereign' (mayor) and the twelve burgesses, as well as picking the two MPs. Some boroughs, such as Carrickfergus and Londonderry, were rather more representative. In the counties the grand juries were responsible for local government; these were made up of the landlords and other leading men of property.

In 1892, R.M. Young edited some of the seventeenth-century records for Belfast in *The Town Book of the Corporation of Belfast*. Most of the records are held in Belfast City Hall and the major task of sorting and cataloguing the archive is now under way in collaboration with PRONI.

EXAMPLE OF EXTRACT FROM LOCAL GOVERNMENT RECORDS

Att an Assembly held for the Burrough aforesaid the XXIX day of March 1638

Fforasmuch as by dayly experience it is founde that mault kills erected in the body of this Towne are very dangerous and enormious and may upon the least accident indanger the whole Towne to be consumed by fyre. It is therefore Ordered and established by the Sovraigne & Burgesses assembled by and with the consent of the Right Honble. Edward Lord Viscount Chichester Lord of the Castle of Belfast, as a by Law p'petually to remayn That from henceforth noe p'son or p'sons inhabiting within the Burrough of Belfaste shall erect or make any mault kill, or make use of any mault kill already erected and built within the said Burrough, but in such convenient places as shalbe allowed of by the Lord of the Castle and the Soveraigne of the Burrough for the tyme being together with syxe of the Burgesses at the least upon pains of forfeiture of five pounds sterl: for every default to be levyd, that shall be presented.

Edward Chichester, Henry Le'Squire Sovraigne, Jo: Leithes, Robt. Foster, John Ayshe, John Wassher

The powers and functions of grand juries were altered and increased; they presided at the assizes and examined bills of endictment and they were given the authority to levy a 'cess' or a rate to build and maintain roads and bridges, award bounties and supervise jails and county institutions. Administrative functions were carried out at presentment sessions. The fullest records survive for the counties of Antrim and Londonderry, and can be found in the Crown and Peace Archive.

EXAMPLES

(ANT/4/1/1) Presentments made at the general sessions of the peace for the aforesaid County [Antrim] held at Carickfergus

9th July 1712

Nomina iurator magnus inquisitionis.

Valutn Jones	Arthur Mathews
Robert Byrt	Mathew Wilson
Thomas Banks	Henry Douglas
Edward Obry	Allexander Acton
Edward Hall	Jon. Cooke
Bryan O'Neille	Ed. Forsayth
Leathes Savage	Jno. Ricie
Cornelius O'Cahane	

£01-03s-10d   One pound three shillings and ten pence off the County at large and paid to William Ross Gaolor for mending locks bolts revelits etc . . .

Tuesday 27th of August in the 11th year of the reign of her Majesty 1712 . . .

Whereas there proceeds from the melting or rendring house of Nicholas Thetford of Belfast chandler the lees dreggs and filth pass from thence into the channell or gutter on the south side of Waring Street alias Bond Street in Belfast and there lyeing or stagnateing occasions a very filthy and vnwholesome stench and is a comon annoyance to all the inhabitants of the said town of Belfast. Weedoe therefore present that the same is a comon nuisance to all the inhabitants of the said town of Belfast . . .

It is this assizes here entered that Mr. Nicholas Thetford of Belfast chandler came voluntarily before this Grand Jury and did promise to remove the above nuisance by carrying the filth that now passes a sink or gutter from his melting house vnder the ground before the latter end of May next then at his own expence provided he be not now prosecuted for the same . . .

[Tedford's remained in business as ships' chandlers on the same site until very recently: with the same name, it is, at the time of writing, an upmarket restaurant.]

£60   Whereas the vpper bridge on Clogh water on the roade from Clogh to Bruaghshane is totally pulled downe by a moste violent rappid flood, we therefore present that the sume of sixty pounds sterling be raised of the County at Large and put into the hands of major Conn Magenis and Roger McCormuck Gent towards the rebuilding of the said bridge. John O'Neill Esquire supervisor . . .

£2   Two pounds to Samuel Duffield on the County for his good service in apprehending of Hugh McLerrnan a horse stealers, who was convicted at last assizes for the same.

. . . 15th of April 1713 . . .

£00-05s   We present the sume of five shillings be raised of the parish of Culfeightrin and payd to James Mac Gown for an otter by him killed in said parish . . .

£02-10s   We present the sume of two pounds ten shillings sterling to be leyed of the County at Large and payd to Andrew Forgison for apprehending and bringing to justice Art O'Hagan a notorious rober and rapparree who was executed this last assizes at Downpatrick, the County of Downe having presented five pounds . . .

By the beginning of the nineteenth century it was becoming increasingly obvious that town corporations were insufficiently energetic in looking after their boroughs but the Tory governments were extremely nervous about extending truly representative institutions across Ireland. Frustrated by the inaction of Lord Donegall, the citizens of Belfast were the first to force the legislators' hands: the very last act of the Irish parliament before its dissolution was to give the town the right to appoint men to look after everyday, humdrum needs such as water supply, policing and street lighting. Newry made similar attempts but failed. Then in 1828 an act enabled leading ratepayers of any town to apply to the viceroy for permission to elect town commissioners to look after paving, lighting, cleansing, and so forth. Towns did not rush to get these new powers for fear of increased local taxes.

In 1830 the Whigs came to power with a different agenda: the Reform

Act was passed in 1832 and in 1840 ten Irish towns and cities acquired representative councils elected by ratepayers. In the countryside ratepayers were able to elect guardians to the boards of the new Poor Law unions, but the men of property stayed in control of the counties. Gradually more towns applied to have town commissioners, a process eased by further legislation in 1854.

Dungannon received the right to have town commissioners in 1834 but it was not until 1843 that records appear to have been kept:

Commissioners' minute book (LA/34/2BA/1)

1st August 1843

It was proposed by Mr Thos. Agnew Seconded by Doctor Dawson that Robert H. Bolton Esqr. M.D. do act as Chairman for the ensuing year and unanimously carried . . .

Resolved that the Salary for the Clerk of the Commissioners for the ensuing Year shall be Eight Pounds Sterling . . .

Resolved that Henry Smith and John Hughes be continued Night Watch, for the ensuing year at seven shillings per week each and also a Coat and Hat each to be provided by the Commissioners . . .

7th August 1843

. . . it was agreed upon that a special meeting shall be held on Monday the 14th Inst. for the purpose of receiving tenders for keeping the town clock in repair for the year, also pumps & fountains the cleansing streets lains & alleys for one year . . .

22nd August 1843   Dungannon Augt. 22nd 1843

Gentlemen,

I propose to give you Four Pounds Stg. for the manure of the town, when swept in heaps for one year, providing you will punish as the law directs any person for carrying off same . . .

to the   I am
Board of   Gentlemen
Commissioners   Yours respectfully
                                                           Wm Lilburn

The Dungannon town commissioners' records do not refer directly to the Famine, but it clearly had an impact on the resources at their disposal:

Monday 20th September 1847

In consequence of the embarrassed state of the Funds, the
commissioners have thought it advisable to reduce their expences for
the ensuing year. It was therefore resolved

That the Publick Lamps shall be light in the same manner as last
year and be extinguished every night at 12 o Clock, and that a
Committee be appointed of the following Gentlemen to confer with
the Gas Company in Order to carry out the above resolution, viz

Alexander Russell   Robert Wray   Thomas Kinley
William McClelland & William Holmes Esqrs

It was resolved that no Contract for Keeping in order the Pumps
and Fountains be entered into for the present . . .

The town commissioners in Dungannon were still operating in 1880.
On 8 December they considered a complaint that a very young boy was
being used by the post office to deliver letters. The commissioners

. . . further consider that the employment of a mere lad to such
important work is highly injudicious and may lead to serious
inconvenience and possibly losses. The Commrs. consider that some
person of mature age and of tried character should be entrusted with
the post at a reasonable remuneration for the work as such small
wages are often only an incentive to breaches of duty and fraud.

Representative government was at last brought to the Irish countryside
by the Local Government Act of 1898 which created county councils
elected by ratepayers. Some powers previously held by boards of
guardians were transferred to these new bodies and the grand juries
were swept away. Northern Ireland inherited this structure in 1921 and
the functions of local authorities increased only slowly in the inter-war
years. The introduction of the welfare state immediately after the
Second World War massively increased the functions of local authorities and the sums available to them. Discontent with these local
authorities and the way in which they carried out their duties was a
potent cause of the civil rights movement in the 1960s. In urban areas
ratepayers had been able to vote with a standard franchise since 1840
and as prosperity increased more people won the right to vote. Secret
ballot was introduced throughout the United Kingdom in 1872; until
then, how men voted was public knowledge in both parliamentary and
local government elections. A huge amount of energy was expended in
attempting to disqualify men known to be political opponents and to

get the vote for known allies.

In 1938 Northern Ireland had six county councils, two county borough councils, three borough councils, thirty urban district councils, thirty-two rural district councils, three town commissions and twenty-seven boards of guardians – all these served a population of a mere one and a half million people and, what is more, they were responsible only for 14 per cent of domestic expenditure in 1929–30, compared with 39 per cent in Britain. Yet it was gross mismanagement in this sphere which was the cause of so much tension.

Sweeping changes followed the suspension of Stormont in 1972 and the implementation of the recommendations of the 1970 Macrory Report in 1973: the creation of twenty-six district councils and two city councils and the drastic reduction in the powers of local authorities – powers redistributed to appointed boards and to central government.

Group photograph, *c.* 1926, featuring Sir James Craig, later Lord Craigavon (sixth from left), from the business records of John Kirk, grocer and hardware merchant, Antrim town, *c.* 1900–60 (identity of the rest of the group is unknown)

D/3454/4

10
LOCAL ASPECTS OF
CENTRAL GOVERNMENT RECORDS

When Northern Ireland was established in 1921 the new constitutional arrangements were described by the Presbyterian home ruler, the Reverend James Armour of Ballymoney, as 'a form of Home Rule that the Devil himself could never have imagined'. In the 1960s the English historian, A.J.P. Taylor, referred to the Government of Ireland Act of 1920 as 'an arrangement of fantastic complexity'. The reality was that the amount of freedom of action allowed by the devolutionary arrangements was strictly limited, particularly on expenditure. In any case Northern Ireland is a small place and Northern Ireland government departments found that much of their energy was absorbed by local and often petty matters. In short, the local historian should be prepared to find highly relevant material in central government records.

It would seem surprising that the office of prime minister should be a place to start investigation, but the first premier, Sir James Craig (Lord Craigavon from 1927) was intensely interested in minor local affairs and, to the frustration of his senior civil servants, would meet delegations more appropriate to a county council and correspond on minor personal matters. There are around four thousand PM/ files and a great many of these, particularly before 1940, deal with issues of interest to the local historian.

Members of the public frequently wrote to the prime minister asking him to use his influence to get them jobs – and sometimes they were successful. This letter is typical (PM 2/3/1/1–10):

J. CADDEN   26 Campsie Road, Omagh
                                                   6/7/23

Sir,

The Postmastership of Portrush has again been announced as vacant and I am a candidate for the position. As you are aware on the last occasion on which the office was vacant I was a candidate, and in verbal conversation in the British Legion Club rooms here you were in agreement that it was most unfair that a man from the Free State should have been appointed. You, Sir – further stated that it would only be a pleasure to assist me should I become a candidate for a similar position. As a loyal subject of H.M. the King and Empire, a disabled ex-serviceman, and an official with upwards of 20 years service with unblemished record I again appeal for your valuable influence* please*

                         I am Sir
                         your obedient servant
                         J. Cadden

Rt Honbl Sir J. Craig et.

Letters from a Church of Ireland clergyman, J.R. Macdonald of Donaghcloney, County Down, absorbed a good deal of energy in the civil service, partly because the correspondent was a leading member of the Orange Order:

REV J.R. MACDONALD   Donaghcloney Rectory
                                                      Waringstown
                                                      6 August 1930

Dear Lord Craigavon,

The Dean of Down has asked me to bring the following Mixed
Marriage before the Orange Order to see if anything can be done in
the matter, or to have steps taken that a similar case will not occur
again. As the marriage took place in Downpatrick [Craigavon's
constituency] I am passing on the facts to you.

A youth named Harry Aage (18 years of age & a member of the
Church of Ireland) was married to a Roman Catholic girl of full age at
about 9 o'clock in the evening in Downpatrick R.C. Chapel about
May 1930.

The father of the bridegroom was a soldier who was killed in the
war. Before the marriage took place the bridegroom's mother went
personally to the priest & warned him that her son was under age &
not to perform the ceremony . . .

The mother it seems, is heartbroken over it & is very bitter about
the indifference & impotence of Protestants.

Yours fraternally,

J.R. Macdonald

The letter was acknowledged by C.H. Blackmore, the prime minister's
secretary, who passed it on to the permanent secretary at the ministry
of home affairs, Major G.A. Harris, CBE, DSO. Harris replied with a long
letter, agreeing that it was against the law for a priest to marry a
Protestant to a Catholic after 2 p.m. but concluding:

The time factor disabilities referred to above do not apply in the case
where the non-Roman Catholic referred to has even immediately
prior to the marriage been admitted into the Roman Catholic Church
and apparently a Protestant can be admitted into the Roman Catholic
Church one day and married to a Roman Catholic the next without
any statutory restriction . . .

Macdonald replied angrily from his holiday address, the Royal Portrush
Golf Club, on 3 September 1930, emphasising that no mention had
been made of the boy's age and adding:

His mother's nearly distracted about it, and the Catholics are in fact jeering at the impotence of us Protestants . . . The Roman Catholics, who are shouting that they are persecuted in the Six Counties, can do what they like and are responsible to nobody . . .

The prime minister now became personally involved and arranged that his minister of home affairs, Sir Richard Dawson Bates, would give Macdonald an interview. Blackmore wrote to Macdonald on 8 October 1930:

The Prime Minister suggests that the next time you are in Belfast you could perhaps call and have a word with Sir Dawson Bates . . . it is understood the youth referred to voluntarily embraced the Roman Catholic faith before the marriage took place, and if this is so you will realise the great difficulty . . .

Correspondence of a similar nature can be found in the records of government departments from 1920 onwards, including home affairs, finance, commerce, agriculture, and health and local government. Departmental records, listed in the brown calendars, are in fact as voluminous as privately desposited material at PRONI.

Warrenpoint and Rostrevor Tramway Company 'longcar' at Greencastle Point, Kilkeel, County Down, c. 1900   D/2050/4

11
TRANSPORT

PRONI possesses extensive records on aspects of transport in Ulster. Surviving grand jury and other local government records from the early eighteenth century onwards demonstrate how, in the long period of peace after the Williamite Wars, the maintenance and construction of roads no longer became the sole concern of local farmers and landowners. From 1615 it was the duty of parishes to repair roads: every farmer owning a plough had to contribute a cart and horses, together with four men, and poorer tenants and labourers were bound to attend in person for six days. From 1710 county grand juries could levy a cess, or local rate, to make new roads. Turnpike trusts could be set up from 1733. The Irish parliament frequently debated transport issues and passed over full responsibility for road building to all grand juries in 1765, ending unpaid six-day labour and subsidies to turnpikes.

Turnpike charges and increases in cess led to local disturbances: bands of weavers and farmers, calling themselves 'Hearts of Oak', tore down toll gates and resisted cess collectors. The turbulence in County Armagh had to be quelled by the army in 1772.

Grand juries were not removed until 1898 but long before then road building had become the responsibility of town commissioners, municipal corporations and the board of works. The Irish parliament directly involved itself in inland navigation from the outset and regularly voted large subsidies to canal companies. In 1729 parliament set up the Commissioners for Inland Navigation for Ireland and levied duties on luxury goods to provide the new body with funds. The Newry Navigation, completed in 1742, was the earliest true summit-level canal, pre-dating both the Sankey Cut at St Helens and the Bridgewater Canal to Manchester. The Lagan Navigation, begun in 1756, extended from Belfast to Lisburn by 1763, and reached Lough Neagh by 1793. The extension of inland waterways in the nineteenth century west of the River Bann yielded poor returns, even with considerable government subsidy. The Ballinamore and Ballyconnell Navigation, opened in 1860, was a failure from the outset.

Ulster's first railway, from Belfast to Lisburn, was formally opened on 12 August 1837, and by 1842 the line had reached Portadown. Railway companies had to get parliamentary permission but did not receive aid from the public purse until Conservative governments, attempting to 'kill home rule with kindness', subsidised light railways in the west in the closing years of the nineteenth century. By the early twentieth century Ireland had a highly sophisticated transport network – vastly superior, for example, to that in Scotland – connected to the rest of the United Kingdom by steamship services across the Irish Sea.

The political division of the island in 1921 resulted in a new frontier sweeping through roads, canals and railways but the dislocation was less than might have been expected. By then motor transport was beginning to challenge rail though the Northern Ireland Railway Commission concluded in 1922 that 'motor transport, so far as can be seen, is more likely to become an auxiliary than a competing factor to be economically reckoned with'. Ten years later this prediction had been proved to be false, and in 1935 the government amalgamated all public road transport. In 1948 the Northern Ireland Road Transport Board was integrated with nationalised railways to form the Ulster Transport Authority. The ministry of development henceforth had overall charge of the region's transport system until the introduction of direct rule in 1972.

EXAMPLES OF RECORDS RELATING TO TRANSPORT HELD IN PRONI

Papers of the Bessbrook and Newry Tramway Company, including lists of shareholders, receipt books and lists of excursion fares from Bessbrook to Warrenpoint, Rostrevor and Omeath, February 1885–September 1910 (D/2368/1–6)

Petition for a new roadway by the inhabitants of Moy, County Tyrone, to magistrates and cess payers in 1842 (D/1806)

Annaghmore Railway, County Armagh: daily account book (1865–67), kept by J.P. McGilly, wine and spirit merchant, on purchases made by railway workers (D/1849/1/3)

Plan of the Ballyshannon extension of the Donegal Railway c. 1900 (D/2511/5/2)

Ministry of home affairs file on the Belfast–Holywood by-pass road and Tillysburn underpass in 1938 (HA/20/A/81)

Plan of a new road from Tandragee to Lurgan in 1835 (D/2027)

Tenders for the maintenance of roads in the Downpatrick area in 1845 (D/2577)

Papers from the Ulster Canal Company and lands at Keshabouy, County Armagh, 1834–? (D/2027)

Printed acts on the Ulster Canal to be built from Lough Erne, County Fermanagh, to the River Blackwater in County Armagh, 1825–1841 (D/2966/29/1)

Records of the Ulster Transport Authority, including papers on railways, tramways, bus companies, hauliers, carriers, shipping companies and airports, 1820–1976 (UTA)

Papers of Victor S. Kingsmill, engineering draughtsman, Belfast, 1898–1925 (D/1740)

Log book of the voyage of the barque *Forest Queen* from Belfast to Miramichi Bay, Canada, in 1883 (D/2015/1/3)

Around thirty letters, 1935–50, to Captain R.H. Davis from friends and old seafarers on their experiences on the sea and the vessels they knew – subsequently used by Davis in BBC talks given between 1936 and 1955 (D/2015/3/2)

Papers of the Irish Shipowners' Company, 1890–1, including a damp press outward letter book on ships and the selection of crews (D/2015/6/1)

The Clogher Valley Tramway and Great Northern Railway timetable of summer excursions to Bundoran, 1 May–31 October 1899

(D/2567/4A)

Elevations and sections of a jetty in Truagh Bay, County Armagh, surveyed by R.H. Dorman, August 1907 (D/2567/14)

Schedules of road lengths and road expenditure by county and borough councils, 1920–2 (COM/70/3)

Papers on the purchase of land for the Portadown and Dungannon Railway in 1852 (D/1754/15)

Photographs of work on the Toome–Hillhead road, County Londonderry, 1928–9 (D/2561/19–20)

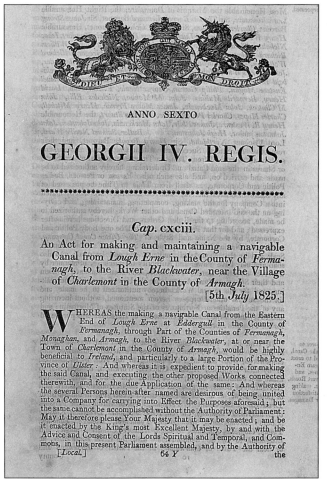

D/2966/29/1

Opening page of a volume of printed acts (1825–41) relating to the building of the Ulster Canal from Lough Erne, County Fermanagh, to the River Blackwater, near Charlemont village, County Armagh

Interior of John Kirk's grocery shop, High Street, Antrim, *c.* 1900   D/3454/3

12
BUSINESS RECORDS

Business and commerce did more than anything else to raise Ulster from being the poorest province in Ireland to being, for some time, the most prosperous. The role of linen was central in quickening the pace of change. The Irish had made linen from very early times but the cloth was too narrow in width to be suitable for export. Planters from the north of England put manufacture on a commercial footing and Huguenots brought over the Jacquard loom and other new technology. The high density of the rural population in central Ulster and the high rents for land there are largely accounted for by the domestic manufacture of linen by farmer–weavers in the eighteenth and early nineteenth centuries.

Literate though many of the weavers were, most of the linen records for the eighteenth century come from drapers, those who bought, washed, beetled, bleached and marketed the cloth. Landlords, such as the Brownlows of County Armagh, were eager to encourage the industry and set up markets to augment their income, and therefore landed estates records can be of great value in tracing the history of the domestic linen industry.

Water and steam-powered technology promoted concentration. The cotton industry flourished briefly in Belfast, to be replaced in the 1830s by the power-spinning of flax; the power-weaving of cloth followed from the 1850s, making Belfast the world centre of the linen industry by the end of the 1860s. The extension of the railway network brought coal and imported flax to other centres in the Ulster countryside such as Gilford, County Down, and Sion Mills, County Tyrone. In addition a shirt industry developed in Derry city and its environs.

PRONI has business records for more than 250 linen companies, many dating back to the eighteenth century. The range of material is very wide, including account books, ledgers, information on customers and suppliers, wages books, technical papers and correspondence. Unlike shipbuilding and engineering concerns, many linen firms built houses for their workers – in some cases, such as Bessbrook and Gilford, entire villages – and therefore business records can yield some unexpected details on a locality.

The linen industry enjoyed a great boom during the American Civil War and remained the main employer of industrial labour into the 1950s. Thereafter it suffered a near-terminal decline, which partly explains why PRONI possesses so many complete records of linen firms.

EXAMPLES FROM LINEN BUSINESS RECORDS

> An account book, 1751–4, giving details of the purchase of brown (unbleached) linen – yarn which was bought in Inishowen, County Donegal, and put out through middlemen to cottage weavers at Ballyrashane; author unknown (T/1044)

> A linen merchant's diary giving an account of travelling on business between Belfast and Liverpool in 1779; author unknown (T/1763/3)

> Around a thousand letters of business correspondence of the owner of a bleach green, Thomas Greer (1724–1803) of Grange, Dungannon, who was in partnership with London merchants and exported cloth from Ulster through Samuel and John Morton of Philadelphia
>
> (D/1044)

The market book of Thomas Greer recording cloth sold to him by various people in different markets, 1758–1803 (T/1127/4)

Deeds, correspondence, accounts, et cetera, of the firm of James Murland, flax spinners and linen manufacturers of Annsborough, County Down (probably the first firm in Ulster to make flax yarn commercially by the powered wet spinning process); papers span the period 1834–1905 (D/1326/8/11–15)

Diary of Henry Jackson Clark, director of William Clark and Sons, linen manufacturers, bleachers, dyers and finishers, of Upperlands, County Londonderry, describing American sales trips and including statistics, accounts, correspondence, et cetera, c. 1900–45 (T/2329)

About a hundred volumes of letter books, invoice books, cash books, journals and ledgers, 1838–1926, from the firm of J. and W. Charley and Company, linen manufacturers and bleachers of Seymour Hill, Dunmurry, County Antrim (D/1171)

Diary giving a day-by-day account of the running of Sion Mills, County Tyrone, owned by Herdman and Company, flax spinners, for the period 1842–6 (T/1650)

Photographs of employees and processes at Sion Mills, c. 1915–c. 1930 (D/1422)

OTHER TEXTILES

Henderson and Eadie, woollen manufacturers, Lisbellaw, County Fermanagh: about 150 volumes and 200 documents, including in-letters, 1836–62; out-letter books, 1919–50; expenditure books, 1860–1934; order books; pattern books; wages books; and correspondence (D/1938)

James Ireland and Company, woollen and worsted manufacturers, 24–8 May Street, Belfast: thirteen photographs showing machinery and weaving processes, 1917 (D/2352)

John McCracken, cotton spinner, Belfast: copy deeds, agreements, correspondence and testamentary papers, 1800–c. 1850. McCracken was brother of Henry Joy McCracken, executed at Belfast's Cornmarket in July 1798 for leading the United Irish rebellion in Antrim. John became a sailor of international standing. Their father, John McCracken, was a ship-owner who imported the first bale of raw cotton into Belfast, and their sister, Mary Ann, ran a muslin business, became involved in the United Irish conspiracy and was a noted defender of women's rights (D/1905/2/40/5).

Samuel Corry and Company, tie manufacturers and hemstitchers, Newtownards, County Down: ledgers, 1910–60; cash books, 1913–41; purchase ledger, 1913–39; invoice books, 1933–8; sales journal, 1913–36; stock book, 1920–56; and correspondence, 1953–6 (D/1965)

The development of the textile industry stimulated the growth of firms manufacturing spinning frames, looms and other powered machines. While water power retained a significant role in the linen industry as late as the 1950s (for example, at Clarks of Upperlands), steam-powered concerns predominated. Mills and weaving factories tended to cluster round the port of Belfast in order to be close to imported cargoes of Scottish and Cumbrian coal at the docks. In 1849 the Belfast Harbour Commissioners completed the Victoria channel to enable large vessels to come up to the quays in all tides; the dredged 'sleech' was dumped close to the south-east shore of Belfast Lough to form Dargan's Island, soon after renamed Queen's Island. It was here that iron shipbuilding began in the 1850s; the engineer Edward Harland in partnership with Gustav Wolff created the flourishing firm which by the end of the nineteenth century had become the largest shipbuilding concern in the world and in January 1899 launched the *Oceanic*, the biggest man-made moving object ever constructed up to that time. The sinking of the *Titanic* on 15 April 1912 severely damaged the firm's reputation but Harland and Wolff retained a pivotal role, particularly as a builder of passenger liners. After the launch of the *Canberra* in 1960, the last great liner to be built in Belfast, the firm became heavily dependent on government support, especially after the oil crisis of 1973–4 when the demand for supertankers plummeted and severe contraction followed.

Harland and Wolff records are divided between PRONI and the NMGNI/Ulster Folk and Transport Museum. The UFTM's collection of ships' plans are not available to the public, and cannot be copied, though the rigging, accommodation and general arrangement plans of the *Titanic* are on public display at the museum. The photographic collection at the UFTM can be consulted. About eight thousand prints of vessels built between 1890 and 1945, bound in volumes, can be viewed in the museum library. There is a card index to those negatives from which prints can be ordered by the public and arrangements can be made to obtain prints from glass plates from which negatives have not been made.

Deposits of business records from Harland and Wolff to PRONI were first made in the 1960s and 1970s (around 16,000 documents and 132 volumes) but, following the publication of the official history, *Shipbuilders to the World* by Michael Moss and John R. Hume, in 1986, files and volumes filling two cars and a van were deposited with PRONI and further deposits were made in the 1990s (D/2805). The immense task of sorting and classification was soon under way and this process is being continually refined.

HIGHLIGHTS OF THE HARLAND AND WOLFF ARCHIVE INCLUDE

The private ledgers of Lord Pirrie, chairman, 1896–1924, which closely demonstrate how the firm responded to booms and slumps experienced by the industry and how Harland and Wolff began to run into financial difficulties after the First World War

Sir Frederick Rebbeck, chairman, 1930–62, left around 100 documents and 57 files including correspondence, technical drawings, annual reports, photographs and newspaper cuttings

The papers of Dr Denis Rebbeck, managing director, 1962–70, which include 962 files of correspondence, notes of meetings, cuttings, et cetera

Fifty-eight files of the personal papers of Sir John Mallabar, chairman, 1966–70

Senior management papers, 1963–77, including minutes, agendas, articles of agreement and technical drawings kept by T.E. Murphy, a former secretary

Extensive technical records, including specifications for contracts

Files dealing with the firm's liaison with trade unions

Records relating to Harland and Wolff's works and premises in Southampton, Clydeside, London and Liverpool

A box of photograph albums showing damage inflicted by German air raids in 1941

The personnel records are, the company states, 'strictly confidential and it is our strict company policy to refuse access for research purposes'. The 'fifty-year rule' applies to the firm's other records, but in practice access can be obtained by submitting a written request which must come through PRONI.

For a comprehensive review of the Harland and Wolff archive consult the PRONI *Statutory Report 1997–98*, Appendix II, written by Dr David Lammey. This can be consulted at the PRONI publications stand in the Public Search Room.

EXAMPLES OF OTHER BUSINESS RECORDS INCLUDE

The papers of Fairbairn, Lawson, Combe, Barbour, Belfast, 1860–1953. This firm owned the important Falls Road Foundry in North Howard Street and made plant and machinery for the preparation and spinning of flax, hemp, jute, silk and other fibres. In 1900 Combe, Barbour and Combe amalgamated with three other companies to form this firm. This archive includes minute books, sales and purchase journals, patents, private in-letters, private out-letters, directors' correspondence, wages books, cash books, accounts and the 1900 Articles of Association. (D/769)

A bound volume list of wheel patterns, et cetera, belonging to John Rowan and Sons, ironfounders, York Street Foundry, Belfast, 1874. This firm invented the piston ring, still in use today. (D/2439/1)

The archive of H. Kennedy and Sons, Coleraine, 1853–86. This firm was one of Ireland's major manufacturers of agricultural machinery in the nineteenth century. This collection consists of an account book of iron foundry fittings, 1853–8, and forty-four bundles of letters relating to machinery and to the iron foundry business received by the firm from various customers and business associates. (D/1036)

Records of the Belfast Ropeworks Company, 1872–1960. Founded largely on the initiative of Gustav Wolff, this company in east Belfast rapidly became the largest of its kind in the world. It supplied half the Royal Navy's requirements in rope and cordage in the First World War and a third during the Second World War. It closed in stages in the 1960s. The archive is made up of ledgers, account books, reports, maps and plans, share ledgers, et cetera. The records are closed for thirty years except for directors' reports and accounts, some photographs, files of press cuttings, and a file for *c.* 1930–70 containing drafts and texts of lectures and articles on ropemaking and the history of the ropeworks. (D/2889)

Records of Messrs J. Cosbie and Company, steam saw mills and coal merchants, Ballymena, 1881–1908. They include copy out-letter books, letters, invoices, order books, day books, catalogues, ledgers and accounts of a provincial firm selling sawn timber, castings, doors, headstones, et cetera. (D/1932)

Boyd and Watts Brewery, Lurgan, 1850–72: the papers of this archive amply demonstrate that records cannot always be fitted neatly into one category. Not only do these papers provide information on a provincial brewery but they also chart the foundation of Lurgan College – included in the will of Samuel Watts in 1850 is the endowment of 'an English Classical and Agricultural School for the education of boys'. The archive contains accounts relating to the brewery, including sundries paid for and stock remaining. The bulk of the papers, however, are connected with the affairs of Lurgan College between 1872 and 1923. (D/3664)

The Londonderry Gaslight Company, 1829–1987: eight minute books (1867–1965) and about 190 other documents including correspondence, maps, newspaper clippings, parliamentary legislation, photographs, publications and registers – D/3806/2/2, for example, is a bundle of around thirty assignments, contracts and mortgages.

(D/3806)

13
SOLICITORS' RECORDS

Proni holds records of more than 140 Northern Ireland solicitors' practices. As industry and trade developed, and agriculture became more commercialised, so the role of the solicitor was enhanced, particularly after the 1881 Land Act which introduced judicial rents and the later land purchase legislation. Those records concerned with the administration of solicitors' offices are of interest only to researchers investigating the development of law firms in Northern Ireland. Clients' papers, however, include much valuable local information on businesses, property owners and economic activity in general.

EXAMPLES FROM SOLICITORS' RECORDS

Messrs Heron and Dobson, Banbridge, County Down. A collection of 551 documents dating between 1713 and 1928, this is made up of leases, titles and testamentary deeds concerning lands in the eighteenth century; bank and expenditure books; and wills and mortgage agreements primarily for lands in mid and west Down.

(D/1046)

L'Estrange and Brett, Belfast. This is by far the most impressive archive from the east of Northern Ireland. It includes papers on distillers, flax merchants, linen manufacturers, chemical works, Belfast Improvement Schemes and the Belfast Philharmonic Society. (D/1905)

Stuart C. Ross, solicitor, Londonderry city: papers extending from 1903 to 1960, with entry books giving details of solicitors' attendance on clients and including correspondence and ledgers recording clients' bills, office expenses, et cetera. (D/3723)

The papers of Sir James Emerson Tennent, covering the period 1824–69, form a remarkable archive of interest to local, colonial and international historians. Only a small proportion of the papers can be classified simply as solicitors' records, notably D/2922/F/4. Sir James in his youth fought for the Greeks in their war of independence in the

1820s; deserted the Whigs to become Conservative MP for Belfast in 1832 (the election was a tempestuous one); got the Copyright of Designs Bill through parliament in 1842; acquired the substantial Tempo estate in County Fermanagh through marriage; had a controversial term as colonial secretary in Ceylon; and wrote books on the history of Greece and Ceylon, the capturing and taming of elephants, on natural history and on firearms.

   The papers are comprehensively reviewed in the introduction to the archive, by A.P.W. Malcomson and T.D. McCusker, in the blue D Calendar. (D/2922)

O'Rorke, McDonald and Tweed, solicitors of Point Street, Larne, County Antrim, presented to PRONI the family records of the Johnstons of Glynn. These include: a family bible endorsed with particulars of births, marriages and deaths for the years *c.* 1806–76; a press letter book, 1867–72, concerned mainly with lime quarries; photograph albums of the late nineteenth century from South Africa and India (at the time of the Afghan Wars); and the Reverend Dr William Corkey's strongly worded denunciation of 'the government's proposals to repeal and nullify the guarantee for Bible Instruction contained in the Education Act N.I. (1930) . . . ' (D/1783)

Messrs Murland and Company, solicitors, Downpatrick, deposited around sixty documents relating to the Duke of Manchester's County Armagh estate, to the Obins family property in Portadown, to the Bibby family property in Bishopscourt, County Down, and property in County Cork owned by several families. The earliest document is dated 1687, but most are from the eighteenth and nineteenth centuries and include copy fines, recoveries, deeds of sale, wills and codicils, and receipts. (D/2404)

The free PRONI leaflet, *Local History 6: Solicitors' Records*, can be obtained in the Public Search Room.

Page from the diary of John Galt of Coleraine, 1798

14
JOURNALS AND DIARIES

Perhaps the finest journals have all been published . . . or have they? There is no doubt that the archives contain fascinating, and often colourful and poignant, diaries which give the reader a very immediate flavour of the past. Such documents can provide evidence – social, economic and political – on localities which may be very difficult or impossible to find elsewhere. The quantity, variety and richness of these unpublished manuscripts will be a revelation to all but the most seasoned investigators.

Some were written by visitors, such as the somewhat hypochondrical English clergyman, the Reverend D.A. Beaufort, who wrote a journal of a tour through part of Ireland, 1787–8. Having travelled around Connacht, he entered Ulster at the end of October. On 1 November 1787 he had reached Florencecourt, County Fermanagh (MIC/250):

> Nov. 1st. Drove through the lawn of Florencecourt. The soil is ungrateful and rushy, but Lord Enniskillen improving it very fast . . .
>
> Nov. 2nd . . . Got up pretty easy – was soon attacked with a violent pain in my breast which changed to my back and has now got back to the kidneys and belly but much abated. I all along belch prodigiously . . .
>
> Nov. 3rd. A delightful day . . . Went to see Castle Coole, Lord Belmore's – a fine demesne and exceeding fine gardens, with a pretty lake and a great command of water – which from the place he intends building, seems all connected with Lough Erne . . .

He travelled on to Lowtherstown (now Irvinestown), which he describes as 'a small ugly village' and from there to Dromore, County Tyrone:

> Nov. 5th . . . The inn is a wretched cabin, but annexed to it is a ballroom. All this country, through a chain of naked, unsheltered hills, is all tilled, and produces a great deal of oats, much of which is still in the fields this dismal wet and windy day . . .

That same day he arrived at Omagh:

> This town is frittered among a number of landlords who give no encouragement. The yarn is spun but little woven, all over the country I travelled this day which is thickly peopled. The town is small but stands on two hills, one pretty high, containing little more than one street. The courthouse looks well . . .

He was at Raphoe, County Donegal, on 14 November:

> Dr Knox used to fish on the lake of Templemore by putting a harness on geese, from which he caught many great pike with good diversion, sending the geese first to the other side of the lake in a boat.

On 22 November he visited Shane's Castle, Lord O'Neill's mansion by the north-east shore of Lough Neagh. The species he mentions are still present in the lough: dollaghan, a large lake trout which breeds in the inflowing streams; and pollan, a white fish found nowhere else in the world, at one time thought to be a kind of freshwater herring:

> This lough which is here boundless to the eye, is agitated like the tide of the sea and abounds (I hear) with fish. Indeed, I saw poles for drying their nets. Trout are plenty and particularly a white fish called pullens – there are also very large trout called dolaghans. Saw a few boats at anchor but none navigating the lough from whence there is a canal to Antrim, much out of repair.

A detailed diary kept by John Galt of Coleraine between 1796 and 1824 is a unique and under-used source which opens a fascinating window on a turbulent period in north Antrim. His journal illustrates the impact of the evangelical revival, for he was a devout and active member of the Methodist Society in the town. Like nearly all Irish Methodists at the time, he was politically conservative, a supporter of the Crown, law and order, and utterly opposed to the United Irishmen who were so active in this district.

On 30 May 1798 Galt reports the outbreak of rebellion but actually the insurrection, which started in Leinster on 23 May, did not erupt in Ulster until the last hours of 6 June in Larne (D/561):

> Alas! what we justly feared, is now approaching, the county of Antrim, in different parts, is quite in a state of rebellion. Belfast is much blamed, as being the nursery of it in Ulster; several persons of distinction have been taken up there . . . From the large military force of local and other troops in our town at present, and Colerain being made the Garrison Town for an extensive circuit, under the command of Lord Henry Murray, we hope through the divine blessing of his military wisdom that he will be our human Saviour . . .

On 8 June he got news of the Battle of Antrim:

> A severe contested battle was brought on yesterday in Antrim, between the troops and the insurgents . . . [He reports the death of Lord O'Neill in the fighting.] . . . Alas! who should put confidence in an infuriated mob. Since the triumph of the rebels in Antrim, they are come ten miles near us, and are now in possession of Ballymena. Yet after all, the Lord still reigneth, though the earth be ever so unquiet.

Note that he believed the insurgents had won in Antrim, though they remained in control of Ballymena, and he is therefore deeply grateful that Coleraine is still in government hands on 9 June:

> Everlasting honor and praise be unto my exalted interceding Saviour. I can yet sing Hallelujah to God and the Lamb . . . The rebel army, after leaving their garrison in Ballymoney, which they are now in possession of also, and within six miles of us . . .

On 11 June 1798 Galt records Lord Murray's success in forcing the insurgents to retreat and disperse:

> With grateful songs of praise to our God and Saviour, I take up my pen this evening. Since Friday, the 8th, this Town has been, from, on the high road of hope, to the low valley of despair. On Saturday morning, the drums beat to arms, it is easier to conceive, than express the sensation that then prevailed among the classes of the people. Lord Henry Murray . . . marched at the head of his troops to Ballymoney to attack the enemy on their own ground . . .

He describes the government victory and the first execution of an insurgent in Coleraine: 'He was a member of the Methodist Society in Ballymoney, but that way was too narrow for him, which he forsook, and after this, all the other ordinances of God . . . ' The following year constant bad weather ruined the harvest with the result that God, he believed, 'now threatens us with cleaness of teeth . . . ' On 2 April 1800 Galt, who has nothing to say about the progress of the Union Bill, though the viceroy Lord Cornwallis visited Coleraine, again reported widespread distress:

> How easy it is for God to punish a world, provisions are now got to a melancholy price for the poor.

Robert McElborough, a Belfast gasworker and trade union activist, wrote a memoir which is largely concerned with disputes within the trade union movement but also contains vivid accounts of his experience at National School and of political violence in the city. In this extract he describes conditions in east Belfast:

> I was taken off the meter work and was told by the superintendent to keep the lamps in Seaforde Street and the Short Strand in repair . . . This was in 1922, and anyone who lived in the area remembers the cross-firing that was kept up day and night . . .
>   I can't tell how I got the cart into this area. I ran with it and got safely into Madrid Street and Seaforde Street with rifles cracking overhead . . . there was times when I had to clear out, when someone

who lived in the district had been shot by a sniper. It was the snipers
on the roofs and back windows who were the danger. Anyone seen on
the streets within the range of their gun was their target, and they
found out later through the press what side he belonged to. I had seen
men who were going to work shot dead as a reprisal for some other
victim. My only dread was when I was standing on the ladder putting
up a lamp, bullets that I suppose were meant for me went through the
lamp reflector . . .

Some of the finest diaries and journals held in PRONI were written by
women. Perhaps the most important are the diaries of Emma Duffin,
daughter of the Liberal Unionist MP, Adam Duffin, and direct descen-
dant of Dr William Drennan, founder of the United Irishmen. She was
a volunteer nurse in France during the First World War and again during the German air raids on Belfast in 1941.

In this extract she describes conditions at Le Havre in July 1916 after
the start of the Battle of the Somme (D/2109/13):

I had not been on night duty very long when the big push began and
the trains came and came, and the boats did not come fast enough,
and we worked all night and came on duty again after breakfast and
prayed and looked for the boats . . . I was sent on duty on the station
platform; if the hospital had not made me realize the war I realized it
that night; under the big arc lights in the station lay stretchers 4 deep
. . . I was up and down all night feeling I was in a bad dream . . .
feeling the pulses of men who felt faint, rearranging a bandage that
had slipped and watching for haemorrhages . . .

On 16 April 1941 she saw at least 250 corpses laid out in Belfast's St
George's Market after the Easter Tuesday German air raid:

No attendant nurse had soothed the last moments of these victims, no
gently reverent hand had closed their eyes or crossed their hands.
With tangled hair, staring eyes, contorted limbs, their grey-green faces
covered with dust they lay bundled into the coffins, half-shrouded in
rugs or blankets or an occasional sheet, still wearing their dirty, torn,
twisted garments . . .

The diaries of Lillian Spender give a vivid impression of what it was
like to be a female member of the middle classes in Ulster during the
first half of the twentieth century. She was married to Wilfred Spender,
an English army officer who resigned his commission to help the Ulster
Volunteer Force just before the First World War, who served with the
36th (Ulster) Division during the war, and who became secretary to the

Northern Ireland cabinet in 1921. Lilian appears to have adored Ulster (Protestant Ulster, it must be admitted) almost from the moment she arrived; she certainly adored her husband (always referred to as 'Wolf' in her diaries); and she was not afraid to confide to her diary when she was bored by the company she was in or when she had to endure what for her was the repellent company of Richard Dawson Bates, minister of home affairs, 1921–43. Her diary is particularly valuable on the campaign against the Third Home Rule Bill, on the involvement of Ulster in the First World War, and on the turbulent period when Northern Ireland came into being.

Here her diary describes the gun-running for the UVF on 24–5 April 1914 (D/1633/2/19):

> W. had told me he would have to be away that night with the General, seeing after the big Test Mobilisation which was to take place then, but which was being kept a profound secret until the last moment . . . His post was to be at Musgrave Channel, assisting at the Hoax which took in all the Customs officers, & kept them occupied all night, watching the 'Balmerino' which of course contained nothing but coal! . . .
>
> I was anxious, & we occupied ourselves as best we could, by catechising one another in First Aid & Home Nursing . . . The whole proceedings are almost incredible, and nothing but the most perfect organisation, combined with the most perfect and loyal co-operation on the part of all concerned, could have carried it through without a single case of bloodshed. Need I say that for the organisation W. himself was mainly responsible, the scheme having been originally drawn up by him?

On 6 May 1914 she attended the presentation of UVF colours at Glencairn in north Belfast:

> The presentation was to the first and second battalions of the West Belfast regiment, and they all marched past afterwards.
>
> It is a beautiful ceremony. The officiating person offers some prayers and blesses the Colours, and one or two speeches are made, and then several men of the regiment come forward and kneel on one knee to receive the Colours, and then march proudly away with them to the tune of God Save the King. The West Belfast regiment is the poorest of all, I mean its men are of a lower class than the others, as they are all in Devlin's constituency which is the slummiest in the city. Many of the men looked just the type you see loafing about public houses,

have to be away that night with the General, seeing
after the big Test Mobilisation which was to take place
then, but which was being kept a profound secret until
the last moment. He left soon after lunch, taking
a Latch Key, as he said it was possible he might get back
early Saturday morning. Eva & I had a busy afternoon,
bandaging each other &c., & Mrs Johnson & a Cousin
turned up to tea. When they'd left, we flew off to
the 'Drill' at the O.T.H. Jack was able to come, &
gave us a splendid drilling, both Stretcher Drill, &
ordinary. We really are improving. We were all
wondering if we were to mobilise too, but had had
no orders so concluded we weren't wanted. Jack
came away with Eva & me, & managed to tell me in
a hurried aside, that "they" were to "get them in
tonight". Of course I knew what that meant, & so will
you, in the light of Saturday's evening papers. His
post was to be at Musgrave Channel, assisting at
the Hoax which took in all the Customs Officers, &
kept them occupied all night, watching the 'Balmer'
which of course contained nothing but coal!
You can imagine my anxiety, realising what was
afoot & what the dangers were & not in the least
knowing what part W. was taking in the night
proceedings. I could not tell Eva, but she knew
I was anxious, & we occupied ourselves as best
we could, by catechising one another in First

Page from the diary of Lillian Spender (later Lady Spender)   D/1633/2/19
                                                                      (page 33)

and were no better dressed, but they marched every bit as well as the
others . . .

Lady Cecil Mary Craig had a similar background to that of Lillian
Spender: she was the English wife of Sir James Craig, first prime minister of Northern Ireland (1921–40, Lord Craigavon from 1927).

In this extract from her journal, she describes the visit of George V to
Belfast to open the Northern Ireland parliament in 1922 (D/1415/B/38):

Jun. 22. The great day, (22, again!). The King and Queen have the
most wonderful reception, the decorations everywhere are extremely

well done and even the little side streets that they will never be
within miles of are draped with bunting and flags, and the pavement
and lampposts painted red white and blue, really most touching, as a
sign of their loyalty. Imagine Radicals in England thinking they would
ever succeed in driving people like that out of the British Empire, or
wanting to! J. goes to the Docks of course to meet them and gets a
great welcome from the enormous crowds everywhere along the route
. . . The actual Opening was the first part of the functions, after which
the boys and I were taken along to the Parlour, and I went in to be
received by the Queen, who told me they were quite astounded by
their welcome, Pi had previously presented her with a bouquet. The
boys and Jimmy Hamilton went in to be presented to the King, who
said he had heard from the Head Master at Eton, that he had given
them leave to come over. He also said to our Jimmy, that it was very
unfair of him to be much taller than his brother when they were
twins . . .

The best-known Ulster woman from the eighteenth century is
undoubtedly Mary Ann McCracken, but a woman who was as politically aware and as independent-minded was Mary Ann's contemporary,
Martha McTier, sister of Dr William Drennan and wife of Samuel
McTier, both of whom were key founders of the Society of United
Irishmen in 1791. She conducted a long correspondence with her
brother, who was often away from Belfast.

In this letter to Dr Drennan she describes the sudden government
crack-down on the United Irishmen in Belfast on 16 September 1796
(D/591/640):

> Since ten o'clock this morning Belfast has been under military
> government. A troop of horse is before my door. A guard on Haslett's,
> which is near us. One at Church Lane, the Long Bridge and every
> avenue to the town. Haslett is taken; Neilson and Russell have been
> walking the streets till about an hour ago, when the Library being
> broken open and a search made for them they delivered themselves
> up, with one Osborne, Kennedy, printer at the Star office, one
> Shannon, young Teeling taken, I am told, by Lord Castlereagh,
> with several more in Lisburn.

For a picture of Northern Ireland just before and during the Second
World War it is most rewarding to consult the journal kept by Moya
Woodside, a surgeon's wife living in south Belfast and a reporter for the
Tom Harrisson Mass Observation organisation.

In these extracts she describes the situation immediately following

ADOLF HITLER

BERLIN, DEN 2. April 1936.

Sehr verehrte Lady Londonderry !

Nehmen Sie bitte für die Übersendung des Bildes und der reizvollen Liedersammlung mit den schönen alten Melodien meinen herzlichen Dank entgegen.

Es war mir eine besondere Freude, aus Ihren begleitenden Zeilen zu ersehen, ein wie grosses Verständnis Sie und Ihr Gatte meinen Bemühungen um einen wahrhaften Frieden entgegenbringen. Ich möchte auch Ihnen für die schöne und dankbare Aufgabe, die Sie sich selbst gestellt haben, aus aufrichtigem Herzen Erfolg wünschen.

Mit den besten Empfehlungen an Ihren Gatten und mit ergebensten Grüssen

Ihr

Marchioness
of Londonderry,
Londonderry House
Park Lane.

Letter from Adolf Hitler, Berlin, to Lady Londonderry, 2 April 1936   D/3099/3/35/9A

Dear Lady Londonderry,

Please accept my warmest thanks for sending me the picture and the charming collection of songs with the beautiful old melodies.

I was particularly overjoyed to learn from your accompanying letter how much you and your husband sympathise with my efforts to bring about a genuine peace. I would like also, with all my heart, to wish you success in the noble and beneficent task that you have set yourself.

With kindest regards to your husband and with respectful greetings.

A. Hitler

the German air raid on Belfast on 15–16 April 1941. She watched an exodus on foot, trams, lorries, trailers, cattle floats, bicycles, delivery vans, anything that would move was utilised (T/3808):

> Private cars streamed past . . . all sorts of paraphernalia roped on behind. Hundreds were waiting at bus-stops. Anxiety on every face . . .

Shortly afterwards she got an account from her sister, who lived in the countryside, of the impact of urban evacuees: she complained of

> the appalling influx from the slums the day after the raid. They were totally unprepared for such numbers and the type of people arriving. The whole town is horrified by the filth of these evacuees and by their filthy habits and take-it-for-granted-attitude . . . The smell is awful . . . They don't even use the lavatory, they just do it on the floor, grown-ups and children.

An example of an unpublished memoir is that of Dr Florence Stewart (known to all as Hazel) who was a medical student at Queen's University Belfast from 1927 and a general practitioner in the city after graduation. Her observations on the Medical School at Queen's are interesting – one of her teachers was Professor Flynn, father of the film actor Errol Flynn – and, at a local level, she charts progress made in medical practice from the 1930s to 1970 (D/3612/3/1):

> Needles were tested before boiling to see if they had developed a hook by drawing them across my thumb nail – the advent of sterilised syringes and needles made such a difference . . .
>
> The best 'champ' I have ever tasted was in a kitchen house on the Shankill, the best white bread and butter was in a kitchen house in the Falls . . .

Papers relevant to women's history are to be found scattered throughout the major collections at PRONI, many of them in the form of correspondence, and include items on: education; clubs and societies; women in politics; women at war; health; household and family; travel and emigration; the arts and entertainment; crime and punishment; religion; social mores; employment and manufacture; trade unions; et cetera.

EXAMPLES

Papers of Helen, Lady Dufferin (D/1071/F/A–C)

Letters to Lady Londonderry 1936–39, including some from Hitler, Goebbels and von Ribbentrop (D/1071/35/1–42)

Discussion in the Northern Ireland cabinet on the application of the franchise to women (CAB/4/116–118)

Dorothy Evans and Madge Moore found with explosives for suffragette action in 1914 (BELF/1/1/2/45/8)

The diaries of Charlotte Despard, suffragette and Irish republican (D/2479/1/1–9)

The free PRONI *Guide to Sources for Women's History* can be consulted in the Public Search Room.

Grand Opera House

GREAT VICTORIA STREET, BELFAST.

Proprietors, ...	"WARDEN, LIMITED.'
Managing Director, ...	Mr. FRED W. WARDEN.
Acting Manager, ...	Mr. W. J. ANDREWS.

Week commencing MONDAY, AUGUST 26th, 1901,

MRS. LANGTRY

And ENTIRE COMPANY, SCENERY, DRESSES and EFFECTS,
From the IMPERIAL THEATRE, LONDON,
Under the Direction of Mr. MOUILLOT.

THIS EVENING—

'A ROYAL NECKLACE'

By PIERRE and CLAUDE BERTON.

Count Fersen	Mr JAMES ERSKINE
Louis XVI, King of France	Mr George P. Hawtrey
Cardinal Rohan	Mr W. R. Staveley
Count Cagliostro	Mr David Glassford
Count de la Motte	Mr Hubert Carter
Boehmer, the Jeweller	Mr J. Hurst
Beausire	Mr Arthur Mortimer
Reteaux de Villette	Mr T. Norman Walter
Couut de Province (" Monsieur")	Mr Gilson
Count D'Artois	Mr E. Gard Pye
Duke de Lauzun	Mr Orme Bywater
Count de Polignac ⎱ Courtiers ⎰	Mr Court
Coigny ⎰	Mr Wilfred Holl
Vaudreuil	Mr Randolfe Reade
Dr. Brunier	Mr E. S. Earle
Goupil, a Detective	Mr Challis
A Broom Seller	Mr W. Gayer Mackay
A Chestnut Seller	Mr Lees
A Rat Catcher	Mr George McCloskie
A Pamphlet Seller	Mr Arthur Bowyer
A Savoyard Boy	Mr Criss
Labitte, an Army Clothier	Mr Milton
Dr. Marat	Mr Ernest Maydew
First Sedan Bearer	Mr Vincent
Second Sedan Bearer	Mr Kendal
Sergeant La Rose	Mr Clissop
Officer of the Guard	Mr Lionel Thomas
Servant	Mr Frank M. Cross
Countess de la Motte	Miss Ina Goldsmith
Countess de Polignac	Miss Dorothy Hammond
Duchess de Guemenee	Miss Annie Dwelley
Baronne de Mackan	Miss Maud Bowyer
Mdlle. Bretin, Court Dressmaker	Miss Violet Mervyn
The Dauphin	Miss Winnie Hall
A Stocking Darner	Miss Phœbe Mercer
A Fishwife	Miss Noney Seabrooke

AND

Marie Antoinette, Queen of France ... ⎱ Dual Role ⎰ **Mrs. LANGTRY**
Mlle. Oliva, a Country Girl, a living image of the Queen ⎰

Court Ladies—Miss Helen Antill, Miss Violia Hanston, Miss Mervyn, Miss Marie Masters, Miss Doris Penford, Miss Dudley Melton, Miss Violet Anderson, Miss Wright, Miss Hall, &c. Waiting Maids, Peasants, &c.:—Miss Gertrude Hornby, Miss Mavis Fenn, Miss Gorton, Miss Filby. Miss Moore. Courtiers, Priests, Pages, &c.:—Messrs. Walton, Garnett, Marshall. Frome Audley, Pelham, Marston. Soldiers, Street Boys, Street Vendors, &c.

SYNOPSIS OF SCENERY.

Act 1, Scene 1	ROOM IN COUNT CAGLIOSTRO'S HOUSE.	(Banks)
Scene 2	A STREET IN PARIS. WINTER.	(Joseph Harker)
Scene 3	THE DAUPHIN'S BEDROOM, VERSAILLES.	(Joseph Harker)
Act 2	THE PARK OF TRIANON, VERSAILLES. SUMMER.	(W. Telbin)
Act 3	THE QUEEN'S SALOON, VERSAILLES. THE NEXT MORNING.	(H. K. Browne)
Act 4	AN INN NEAR VERSAILLES.	(W. Telbin)
TIME	JANUARY AND AUGUST, 1785.	

The Furniture supplied by C. Miller & Co., Ltd., High Street.
The Scenery in Act 3 designed by Mr. Frank Verity. Costumes designed and executed by M. Bianchini, of the National Opera, Paris, and Messrs. L. and H. Nathan. Wigs and Head Dresses by Clarkson. The Duel arranged by M. Felix Bertrand. Mrs. Langtry's Dresses by M. Worth, of Paris.

Friday and Saturday—" THE DEGENERATES."

General Manager	(for Mr. Mouillot's Companies) ...	Mr. F. Leslie Moreton
Business Manager ... ⎱ to whom all communications respecting this ⎰	Company should be addressed	Mr. Walner Gregory
Acting Manager ...	Captain Wargrave ⎱ Stage Manager ...	Mr. Arthur Bowyer

During the Performance the Orchestra (under the Direction of Mr. H. A. KNIGHT), will perform the following :—

Overture	"L'Ambassadrice,"	...	...	Auber
" Nell Gwynn " Dances	...	...	...	Edward German
Selection	"Ruddigore,"	...	...	Sullivan
Valse	"Deutsche Lust,"	...	...	J. Strauss
March	"La Ritirata Italiana,"	...	...	Drescher

D/961/1

15
CULTURE, ARTS AND LEISURE

There are many rich veins ready to be quarried in PRONI which could be classified under the heading of 'culture'. References to the theatre in Belfast first appear in the eighteenth century and are frequent in the letters of Martha McTier (Drennan Letters T/765). Early theatre bills for 1805 prove that the renowned English actor, Edmund Kean, worked for several years with a Belfast company. Nineteenth-century theatre bills and posters can be found in quantity under references D/961 and D/1283 in addition to programmes and shows extending over more than 150 years. Amateur drama is most fully documented in the records of the Northern Drama League (D/961) and the Belfast Footlights Amateur Dramatic Club (D/961). Papers from the Ulster Group Theatre, which made such an impact in the post-war years, contributed so notably to BBC radio drama, and produced such actors and impresarios as James Young, Harry Towb, James Ellis, J.G. Devlin and Harold Goldblatt, are classified under D/2435.

EXAMPLES OF THEATRE RECORDS INCLUDE

Dungannon Theatre posters (1809–1923) (T/2591/5, 7–9, 11)

Play entitled *Death at Newtownstewart* by Denis Johnston (the noted producer, director and scriptwriter, and father of the novelist Jennifer Johnston). Written in 1949, the play centres on the trial of T.H. Montgomery for the murder of William Glass, a cashier of the Northern Bank, Newtownstewart, in 1871. (D/1736/23/1)

Programmes for the Abbey theatre in Dublin between 1941 and 1980 (D/3999/4/1)

Programmes for Belfast theatres between 1945 and 1960 (D/2708)

Assignment of share and interest in lease of the Belfast Playhouse, leased to Michael Atkins, comedian, at £7 2s. 0d. per ticket and 4 free tickets in 1799 (D/971/42/C/19)

OPPOSITE: Programme for a production at the Grand Opera House, Belfast, starring Lillie Langtry, August 1901

> Lyric Theatre Papers, including minutes, accounts and correspondence (D/2441)

> Programmes for the Little Theatre, Bangor, County Down, for 1934–5 (D/3999/2/6)

> One folder of minutes of monthly executive meetings, critiques of plays performed, and reports on the annual drama *feis* held by the Northern Drama League from *c.* 1929 to 1936 (D/3070/A/1)

Some very significant material on Ulster writers can be found in PRONI's archives, much of it deposited in recent years. The most important are the private papers of the poets John Hewitt (D/3838) and W.R. Rodgers (D/2833). The Rodgers archive contains 85 volumes, 135 files and 3,000 documents. 'Bertie' Rodgers not only won international attention through his published poetry but also his talents as a scriptwriter and innovative radio broadcaster are still referred to in hushed, reverential tones in the corridors of the BBC. After being ordained, his first 'call' as a Presbyterian minister was to Cloveneden church, Loughgall, County Armagh, where he remained for twelve years. His eloquence is evident in this extract from a sermon, written in pencil on scraps of paper, preached to local Orangemen on the eve of the Second World War (D/2833/A/3/1):

> Whose service is perfect freedom. 'Freedom'. 'Perfect freedom'.
> In these days if you happen to lift up a newspaper very likely the 1st thing that catches your eye will be something maybe about, say, Jews being persecuted in Germany, or Protestant pastors being pushed into prison for what they believe to be the principles of Christ or people being beaten or shot just for speaking against the ruling power. Or maybe you'll read about the number of persons who have committed suicide in Austria rather than face the brutality that was coming to them . . . Yes! And when you have read it all you know that the half of the dreadful truth has not been told. And you lay down your paper and you say to yourself 'Thank God that we live in a free country!' . . . And yet are we not minded to take it too lightly? . . . this freedom which is our very life's blood – it is not a thing that has just dropped into our lap out of the clouds. It is not an accident, a haphazard possession. No! This freedom was wrought for us and bought for us by our forefathers. They won it, inch by inch, they built it, brick by brick . . . We need to remind ourselves that Freedom means struggle, struggle against horrible tyranny . . .

PRONI also holds papers of other Ulster writers such as John Kells Ingram (D/2808), Helen Waddell (T/2043 and T/2508), Dennis Ireland (D/3137), Nesca Robb (D/3847), Mayne Reid (D/2802) and Alexander Irvine (D/2398), as well as letters from Lynn C. Doyle (D/3861), George Shiels (D/1792) and St John Ervine (D/2325). Correspondence from W.B. Yeats, George Bernard Shaw, AE (George Russell), Shane Leslie, Sean O'Casey, Oliver St John Gogarty and others can be found in the Londonderry Papers (D/2846 and D/3099) and the Dufferin Archive (D/1071) holds papers relating to Richard Brindsley Sheridan, Robert Browning and Rudyard Kipling.

MATERIAL ON PICTORIAL ARTISTS, ARCHITECTS, DESIGNERS AND SCULPTORS INCLUDES

Copies of plans and elevations for exhibition on Ulster architecture, 1800–1900 (T/3020)

Forty-five documents on an exhibition of modern Irish religious art and architecture, entitled 'Art in Worship Today', 1967–9 (D/3636; D/3636/1 closed for thirty years)

Christmas card designed by Rosamund Praeger for the Irish women's movement, c. 1914 (D/3155/1)

Letters from the caricaturist John Doyle ('HB') (D/2922/B/10)

Correspondence on the Belfast Art Society (later the Royal Ulster Academy of Arts) with letters from Sir John Lavery and Lord Charlemont, c. 1925 (D/1177)

Talk entitled 'The History of the Ulster Arts Club, 1902–1966' (1967) (T/2644/1)

EXAMPLES OF THE MANY PAPERS RELATED TO MUSICAL EVENTS AND THE ARTS IN GENERAL IS LISTED BELOW

Around a thousand documents on concerts, the Ulster Orchestra, local music and opera societies, and theatrical events in Belfast from 1924 to 1992 (D/3999/3/)

Concert programmes, mainly from Newry, 1906–16 (D/3620)

Annual reports of the Arts Council of Northern Ireland, 1962–89 (AC/2/1)

Programmes for the Belfast Festival at Queen's, 1980–9 (D/3999/3/3)

Programme for an entertainment in the Victoria Hall, Belfast, in 1865 (D/3140/B/2)

Programme for two plays performed by the Gaelic Dramatic Club in the Town Hall, Enniskillen, *c.* 1906 (D/3769/22)

Lithograph of the Old Theatre Royal, Belfast, *c.* 1850 (T/1129)

EXAMPLES OF OTHER ENTERTAINMENTS INCLUDE

Buffalo Bill's Circus and other visiting attractions (D/1422/B/17/26–48)

Entertainments Duty Offence Case: Lurgan Glenavon Supporters' Club and its failure to provide returns of tickets sold (1948–9)
(FIN/15/6/A/6)

File of correspondence with the Picture House, Omagh (D/1736/23/1)

Booklet of lantern lecture entitled 'North of Ireland Holiday on Northern Counties Committee Lines', *c.* 1900 (D/1860/14)

SPORTS RECORDS

The earliest records on organised sport are overwhelmingly connected with hunting, horse racing, beagling, wildfowling and fishing, though in the early seventeenth century the Montgomerys paid the principal master of their school at Newtownards £20 a year 'to teach Latin, Greek and Logycks, allowing scholars a green for recreation at goff, football and archery'. During the nineteenth century, the presence of regular troops in town garrisons and encampments helps to explain the localised nature of enthusiasm for certain sports such as rugby and cricket, and mill owners at Sion Mills, Gilford, Upperlands and elsewhere encouraged the formation of clubs. The Gaelic Athletic Association, founded in 1884, was slow to take off in Ulster but made rapid expansion from the first years of the twentieth century.

PRONI holds, for example, fifty-three volumes of the Irish Football Association's minutes (1880–1985), D/4196 (with restricted access); records of the Northern Ireland Sports Council, SCNI; and papers of the Ulster Women's Hockey Union (1905–93), D/3982; the Ulster branch of the Irish Rugby Football Union (1886–1983), D/3812; and the Northern Cricket Union of Ireland (1914–98), D/4213. Only a flavour of the archive can be given in the list of examples below:

Correspondence and memorabilia of the Route Hunt (1850–65)
(D/1011/10/6)

Hunting diaries of the Earl of Enniskillen (1881–7) (D/1702)

Papers of the Killultagh and Old Rock Chichester Harriers
(1832–1972) (D/3322)

Minute book of the Ballymena Cricket Club (1878–87) (D/1683)

Linfield Football Club papers (1934–72) (D/3852)

Ulster Gliding and Aviation Club, articles of association and
newsletters (1932–9) (D/2498)

Royal County Down Ladies Golf Club papers (1894–98) (T/3796)

Lord Lurgan's greyhound account book (1830–90) (D/1928/A)

Papers of Osborne Hockey Club, Belfast (1909–14) (D/3888)

Letter to the 4th Earl of Antrim with references to horse racing
(1710) (D/2977/5/1)

Letter mentioning trouble at a hurling match at Bushmills,
County Antrim (1910) (D/1006/3/2)

Motor Cycle Union of Ireland minute book (1912–21) (D/3133)

Programme of athletic events and Gaelic games at Celtic Park,
Belfast (1905–10) (D/3864)

Programmes of amateur athletic meetings (1923–8) (D/3325)

Minute book of Newry Rowing Club (1907–35) (T/3147)

Northern Yacht Club minute book (1824–38) (T/3198)

Downshire Lawn Tennis Club papers (1891–1904) (T/819)

Leases of salmon fisheries and fishing rights along the Antrim coast,
granted by the earls of Antrim (1687–1920) (D/2977/3A/7)

Godfrey Brown remembers the beginning of the BBC in Northern
Ireland (1924). He was the first director of music

> I duly reported at 31 Linenhall Street – Then a week or so later the
> Director arrived – Major Walter Montagu Scott . . . his business
> training apparently had been acquired in the orderly room as adjutant
> to a regiment. The Major's first request to me was 'will you please go
> and get two nice and well educated girls as typists and private

secretaries, one for yourself and Mr Thompson and one for me' – He added 'I don't want to advertise, it's such a nuisance sorting them out.' [Evelyn Dales and a Miss Caughey were appointed, and E. Dales was still on the staff in 1949.] Miss Caughey ere long left to be married but her sisters joined and there's always been a Caughey on the staff.

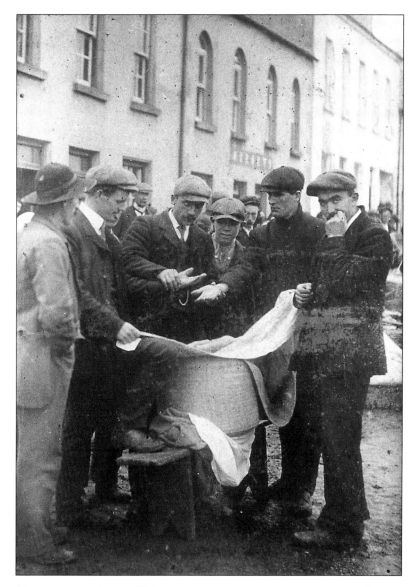

Linen street auction, *c*. 1900

D/2465/1

16
PHOTOGRAPHS

On 6 August 1840 Francis Beatty, a Belfast engraver, announced in the *Northern Whig* that he had made a 'photogenic drawing' or 'calotype' of the Long Bridge. Using a paper negative to produce a positive image on paper, Beatty pioneered photography in Ireland. Wet plates, invented in 1851, led to the opening of many commercial studios (twelve in Belfast and sixty in Dublin by the end of the decade). The need to take cumbersome darkrooms to where photographs were being taken was removed by the invention of the dry-plate process in 1878. By 1881 there were seventy-four professional photographers in Ulster: their work consisted mainly of formal studio portraits, prints of scenery and great houses, stereoscopic views and portraits of notable personalities. The Ulster Amateur Photographic Society was founded in 1885 and in 1888 George Eastman launched the Kodak box camera with the slogan 'You press the button we do the rest', leading to a great increase in family and informal photographs.

Three major collections of photographs of great value to the local historian are held by the National Museums and Galleries of Northern Ireland: the photographs of R.J. Welch, taken from the 1880s to the 1930s, and the Hogg Collection (1901–39), both at the Ulster Museum, Botanic Gardens, Belfast; and the Green Collection, mostly of rural scenes c. 1914–35, at the Ulster Folk and Transport Museum, Cultra, County Down.

The largest collection in PRONI is that of H.F. Cooper, who worked in Strabane, County Tyrone, between around 1908 and 1961. This consists (D/1422) of about 200,000 glass plate negatives, largely of family, wedding and passport photographs but also records events of particular interest to local historians, including political meetings, Ulster Volunteer demonstrations, Orange processions, the Special Constabulary at work, and sporting functions. Life in the counties of Tyrone and Donegal is illustrated by photographs of markets, harvesting, mill and factory interiors, agricultural shows, street scenes, floods in Strabane, railways and circuses.

The Allison family came from Bradford in 1881 and set up in Armagh in 1900, with additional studios in Dundalk, Newry and Warrenpoint, and remained in business until 1953. This large collection (D/2886) includes photographs of streets, historic buildings, outings, churches, country houses, shops, schools, open-air classes in woodwork and poultry-keeping, flax markets, bands and drumming clubs, and political meetings (including one of Michael Collins, subsequently elected MP for Armagh in the first Northern Ireland parliament, at a large Sinn Féin demonstration in the city on 4 February 1921).

Between c. 1890 and c. 1920 W.R. Henderson, a press correspondent and photographer, recorded many scenes and events in Newtownstewart, Plumbridge, Ardstraw, Omagh, Bundoran and other parts of the north-west. PRONI holds around three hundred glass plate negatives and about a hundred prints from his collection (D/2618).

Thousands of photographs are scattered throughout the collections deposited at PRONI. Local landlords were amongst the first amateur enthusiasts and many estates records include nineteenth-century albums. The finest are in the Annesley Papers: Hugh, 5th Earl of Annesley, started taking photographs during his service with the Scots Fusilier Guards in the Kaffir War in 1851–3 and the Crimean War, 1854–6, and eventually filled thirty albums. The photographs not only record the British Army during a period of imperial expansion but also provide a valuable portrait of south County Down in the second half of the nineteenth century. There are few 'action' shots but his lordship showed a considerable talent for composition and witty tableaux.

EXAMPLES OF PHOTOGRAPHS FROM THE ANNESLEY PAPERS

Colonel Henry Ponsonby in a carriage leaving Donard Lodge on 19 February 1857, entitled 'Exit Pon' (D/1854/5/4/69)

The Temple, Castlewellan, County Down (D/1854/5/4/30)

Newcastle Harbour, County Down (D/1854/5/5/24)

'The Great Eastern from Deptford Dockyard', taken on 14 October 1857 (D/1854/5/5/78)

Three women seated on the capstone of Legananny dolmen at the foot of Slieve Croob, County Down (D/1854/5/5/84)

Photographs of Castlewellan Castle under construction (D/1854/5/6)

The Annesley photographs D/1854/5/6/2–7, 9–20, 22–26, 32–33, 36–43 and 45–47 have been copied by the Ulster Museum, and prints are available for consultation under T/3390 and photocopies are kept in the Public Search Room.

Classified under AM/1 are about 60,000 prints, negatives, sortie plots and traces of aerial surveys of Northern Ireland made by the RAF between 1944 and 1959. Around 1,500 prints of air photographs of ring forts, castles, stone circles, mansions and other archaeological and historic features are classified under AM/2.

The government information service has deposited records which include photographs of events such as royal visits and the German air raids on Belfast in 1941 (INF/7).

EXAMPLES FROM OTHER COLLECTIONS

An album, autographed by Thomas McG. Greer in 1882, showing friends and other players at the Killymoon Tennis Club, County Tyrone (D/2829)

A box of loose photographs and an album (c. 1860–1920) showing members of the Moutray and Anketell families of County Armagh, Favour Royal, the Mount Forrest Orange Lodge banner, shorthorn bulls, and the 1st Battalion of the Connaught Rangers in County Westmeath, Malta and India (D/2023/15/1–2)

Thirteen photographs showing the erection of a new factory for Carreras at Seapark, Carrickfergus, in 1965 (D/2566/5)

The annual Christmas poultry show in Crossgar, County Down, in 1894 (D/2357/1)

The interior of Belfast Power Station about 1906, taken by John Beck, junior engineer (D/2373/1)

Album of fourteen photographs of the Belfast Improvement Scheme in 1911, showing slum dwellings in Millfield and neighbouring areas just before demolition (D/2691/1)

Papers of W.J. Kennedy, including photographs of the Royal Irish Constabulary (D/2696)

Photographs deposited by T.J. Wilson of Belfast, which include:

Hariot Georgina, Lady Dufferin, in 1865 (D/2804/3)

Seymour's greengrocery and butcher's shop, Grosvenor Road, Belfast, c. 1910 (D/2804/8)

Twenty-five photographs taken between 1910 and 1920, including the White Star liner *Olympic*, Donaghadee Harbour, crowd scenes at Belfast City Hall, and Shaw's Bridge (D/2804/13/1–25)

Thomas Sexton, Nationalist MP for West Belfast (D/2804/15/10)

A gaff schooner entering Belfast Harbour c. 1900 (D/2804/15/13)

A temperance procession passing Clarke's tailor's shop at the junction of Chichester Street and Arthur Street, Belfast, c. 1910 (D/2804/15/1)

The National Library of Ireland holds the Lawrence Collection which includes over forty thousand views of the towns and countryside of Ireland taken between 1880 and 1914. A thousand of these have been copied and placed in the Ulster Museum and around seven hundred, mostly of the Antrim coast and the Giant's Causeway, are copied in PRONI (T/3680).

The free PRONI leaflet, *Local History 7: Photographic Collections*, can be obtained in the Public Search Room.

17
NEWSPAPERS

Newspapers first appeared in Ireland during the second half of the seventeenth century but, since they were usually issued to cover a particular event, they had brief life spans. The long peace which followed the Battle of Aughrim in 1691 created the settled conditions in which newspapers could circulate freely and find reliable and growing markets. Dublin, the second city of the British Empire in the eighteenth century, naturally was in the van: there Cornelius Carter's *Flying Post* inaugurated continuous newspaper production in 1699 and the leading journal in the country was Faulkner's *Dublin Journal*, published 1719–1825.

In the eighteenth century newspapers were usually issued twice a week, most commonly on Tuesdays and Saturdays to coincide with the days when the post was sent out to the provinces. In 1737 Francis Joy published the first issue of the *Belfast News-Letter*, which eventually became the longest-running provincial newspaper in English in the world. Londonderry began producing newspapers later in the century. These papers can be a little disappointing because most of the news was copied from English newspapers brought across the Irish Sea and the Irish items at first are limited to advertisements and notices of births, marriages and deaths. Circulation was often no more than five hundred copies an issue and advertising was the main source of revenue. Advertisements, however, are often informative:

FATHER O'LEARY

The beautiful and high bred Horse Father O'Leary, will stand this Season at ARMAGH, and cover Mares at the very low price of One Guinea and Half-a-Crown. The money to be paid before service.

O'Leary, when three years old, beat the famous Honest Tom, and was considered the best of his years. He was got by the noted Horse Friar; his Dam, (who was the Dam of the famous Baggot) was got by Eclipse.

The Gets of this Horse are allowed by judges to be much superior to any in Ulster, for fine figure and bone.

April 22, 1797   *Northern Star*

In the second half of the century reports from the Irish parliament are detailed and the government placed proclamations as paid insertions. Local news became more significant, even to the extent of reporting accidents. This is an early example:

BELFAST

On Saturday morning last the Dial-plate of the Market house of this place, fell on a poor labouring man who was then keeping watch, which broke his thigh, and bruised him in so grievous manner, that it's thought he cannot live. 'Tis remarkable that the day before, when a man was on it, it fell not, and yet to have fallen so shortly after.

Belfast News-Letter   15 August 1746

The newspaper was in the process of replacing the pamphlet and was generally a single sheet folded to form four pages. The ferment produced by the American War of Independence and then by the French Revolution increased the demand not only for news but also for radicals, conservatives and revolutionaries to present their views. Perhaps the most successful, and certainly the liveliest, paper of the century was the *Northern Star* published in Belfast from 1792 but circulated throughout the island. In 1796 it ran foul of the authorities and the following year the troops moved in, as this flyer indicates:

In consequence of the Star Office being taken possession of this Morning, by Col. Barber, a King's Messenger, and Military Guard, the Proprietors of the Newspaper have it not in their power to Publish this Day: for this disappointment of their numerous Friends and Readers they are sincerely sorry . . .
   Col. Barber, the Sovereign, and a Military Guard visited Mr. O'Connor's House early this Morning; upon enquiry they found he was not at home: they then searched for and carried off some Papers, and upon their return to Town, arrested Robert and William Simms, the only Proprietors of the Paper now out of Jail – so that independent of the Seizure and Occupation of the Printing Office, by the Officers of Government, the Arrest of these Gentlemen might be sufficient Apology for the want of publication this Day.

BELFAST, Feb. 3, 1797

Shortly afterwards, the Monaghan Militia ransacked the office and threw the type out of the window.
   As the nineteenth century advanced and government fear of

'jacobinism' abated, newspapers increased in size and in circulation, and many new titles appeared. The leap in literacy rates following the introduction of national education in 1831, the abolition of stamp duties and other taxes, and the recovery following the Great Famine, made newspapers a key form of communication. The cost of production was greatly reduced by the introduction of newsprint made from wood pulp in the 1860s to replace the more durable but costlier rag pulp.

Ease of access should not divert the researcher from the fact that for the nineteenth century the newspaper is the most important source for investigating a locality. Of course it is important to find out the political standpoint of the proprietors: the quickest way to do this is to consult *Ulster Politics: The Formative Years, 1868–86*, by Brian Walker (Belfast, 1989, pp. 34–8). Newspapers in the late nineteenth and early twentieth centuries are extraordinarily detailed, reporting meetings, rallies, riots, debates and commercial activities extensively, often providing speeches in full, though usually in reported speech. There are very few photographs and little in the way of moving film on the intense conflict in Ulster between 1920 and 1922 but the newspaper reports are very full and deserve to be drawn upon more frequently. And though the bias of the papers is obvious, the standard of reporting and the quality of writing is generally very high.

When consulting newspapers, remember that those made of wood pulp, particularly for the period 1870–1930, deteriorate rapidly from exposure to light and from slow dissolution owing to the sulphuric acid in the newsprint – for this reason, as many journals as possible are being copied onto microfilm. The comprehensive guide to newspapers in Ireland is *Newsplan: Report of the Newsplan Project in Ireland* by James O'Toole, revised edition by Sara Smith, 1998; this can be consulted in the Public Search Room. This indicates runs and locations (abbreviations are used, such as LHL for the Linen Hall Library, with a key provided).

EXAMPLES OF NEWSPAPERS HELD

Belfast Citizen Daily
  1 August 1886–2 January 1897
  LHL 31 August 1886, 2 January 1897
  PRONI 1 August 1886–December 1886; 5 January 1887–4 May 1887
  Poor, damage to outer margins.

MICROFILM

1 August 1886–December 1886; 5 January 1887–4 May 1887.

PRONI film

Andersonstown News

22 November 1972–

NLI	22 November 1972–
BELB	1978–1972; 1993 imperfect; 1994–
LHL	1972–1982, imperfect, 1983–

MICROFILM

22 November 1972–30 December 1989.

Copy at LHL 1990 – priority 2

Also available in the Public Search Room is *A Guide to Newspapers in PRONI*. Though in recent years PRONI has not accepted newspapers for deposit and has transferred some of its holdings to other institutions, it still has an important selection of Irish newspapers, including some very rare titles such as the *Lisbellaw Gazette*. Runs of newspapers are listed by title; most of the original newspapers are held under the prefix N but individual papers are also included in collections of privately deposited records under the prefix D/ and many titles are available on microfilm, prefix MIC/. Those titles prefaced with an asterix are included in *Newsplan*.

EXAMPLES

* *Belfast Commercial Chronicle*

1806–7, 1813, 1817, 1821, 1832, 1847, 1853	N/7/2
1813–15	MIC/447

Anti-Union [Dublin]

1798–9	MIC/53

ACKNOWLEDGEMENTS

An outstanding characteristic of PRONI is the manner in which all staff, even when under pressure, are unfailingly helpful, courteous and patient in responding to enquiries. Certainly this has been the experience of the author before and during the compilation of this guide. I would like to thank Dr G.J. Slater, Chief Executive of PRONI, for supporting this project. My special thanks go to Dr David Lammey and Heather Stanley, and also to Gerry Drake, Sheenagh Johnston, Alistaire King and Martin Smyth at PRONI; and to Dr W.H. Crawford, Dr W.A. Maguire, Ian Montgomery, Trevor Parkhill and Jeremy Shields. Professional genealogists have an unrivalled and often unacknowledged understanding of sources useful to the local historian and none more so than John McCabe – he would have preferred a guide nine hundred pages long and certainly supplied enough suggestions and references to write such a volume. My thanks also to Joan Petticrew, Jennifer Irwin and Marie Wilson.

JONATHAN BARDON
BELFAST
MAY 2000